CONTENTS

BEFORE YOU BEGIN

So you want to play baseball! Who is going to teach you? Your dad? The kids at school? Your teacher? Your friends down the street? Or will you pick it up the best you can as you watch other boys playing? How do you know you are learning it right?

It is just as easy to learn it right as to learn it wrong, and that is what this book is about. It will tell you, and show you pictures, about how to do some of the things you as a baseball player must know if you are to play baseball well and enjoy it. Each chapter tells about some part of baseball—throwing, hitting, catching, running the bases, sliding, playing the infield, and the outfield. Read each carefully, no matter what position you expect to play on the team. Study the pictures and practice the things you learn.

You can have fun playing good baseball, and it will help keep you healthy, but like anything else, you need to work at it. Practicing just before the game might be a good "warm up" for the game, but it won't help you learn much baseball. You need to warm up every day, even if you do nothing but play catch with your friends or your dad.

Playing good, clean baseball, and having fun doing it is a "warm up" for life. The things you learn will help you to be a healthier, happier person. LEARN IT RIGHT, PLAY IT RIGHT, AND ENJOY IT.

THE CORRECT GRIP for a straight fast throw or pitch. The two fingers on one seam, and the thumb also on a seam, give you control and also give spin to the ball as you release it.

6 ◎ **Throwing**

THROWING

Knowing how to throw a ball is the first thing you must learn if you want to play baseball. This is true for every position on the team. If you can't throw well, you can't help the team. A catcher must throw swiftly to second base. An infielder must throw properly to first base. An outfielder must throw the ball hard in to the infield. So, if you want to play baseball, the first thing is to throw well.

Hold the Ball Correctly

The "stitches" or "seams" which hold the covers on baseballs also help you throw the ball. A ball must "spin" as it goes through the air or it is hard to make it go where you want it to go. Holding the ball with your fingers over the stitches helps give the ball spin as it leaves your hand and travels toward the batter. Put your first and second fingers across the two sets of seams where they come close together. Your thumb must also be on a seam. Practice so that you pick up the ball and hold it this way each time you get it. Hold the ball this way for all throwing and for pitching the fast ball.

SIDE TURNED TOWARD TARGET: This right-handed pitcher is using the set position. Note that his right foot is on the rubber.

Turn Your Side toward Your Target

If you are right-handed, begin your throw with your left shoulder and left leg turned in the direction of your throw. This helps you use the muscles in your shoulders and back to get more power in throwing far or fast. If you should try to throw with your chest facing the target, you will use only the muscles in your arm. Your arm muscles do not have enough power for you to throw very far or very fast. Some pitchers begin their "wind-up" or throwing motion by directly facing the batter with their chest. But before they release the ball on its flight to the plate, they must always turn or twist their side toward the batter so that they can use their shoulder and back muscles. (If you are left-handed, you must "aim" your right side toward the target.)

Step toward the Target

If you are throwing right-handed, your right foot is called the "pivot" foot. When you throw you "push" against your right foot as you step toward the target with your left foot. This step or "stride" can be a big one or a little one. Pitchers take bigger strides than other players do in throwing. In any case, you have to stride as you throw, and you have to turn your body toward the target or hitter at the same time. Practice by drawing a line on the ground between you and your target. As you complete your stride, your left foot should end on the left side of the line.

THE STRIKE ZONE: For practice, hang an old rug, blanket or canvas over a fence or clothesline and outline the zone in chalk.

Letting the Ball Go

As you begin your stride, your right arm should be back and bent at the elbow as you throw. Your hand should come up to within 5 to 8 inches above your ear. Always release the ball at the same place, and from the ends of your first and second fingers. Some boys hold the ball with three fingers, but this is not a good way to do it. It is harder to make three fingers work together than to make two fingers work together. As a result, the ball doesn't go where you want it to go. A good thrower, especially a pitcher, will feel the ball leaving the ends of his two fingers with the tips of his fingers "pushing" on the two seams.

When you are first learning to throw, always throw overhand (arm and hand over and a little to the side of your head). Don't try to throw side-arm (with the ball released from a position lower than your shoulder). As you release the ball, your right foot (pivot foot) should come forward to complete the stride. It should come up to the right of your left foot and even with it. Your right arm should keep on going out and down toward your left foot. This is called "follow-through." You must follow through or your throw will be jerky and may prevent you from throwing straight.

The Strike Zone

If you are below the age of 6, you probably should practice throwing a tennis ball or a rubber ball over

THE SET POSITION: As you begin to pitch, brace your rear foot against the front edge of the rubber and push off.

the plate. By the time you are 7 or 8, you could be throwing a real baseball. But you must practice throwing each day if you want to learn how to throw well.

If you want to pitch, much more practice is needed. There are not many 9-year-old pitchers. Some boys can pitch well by the time they are 10 years old, but most boys can't pitch well until they are 11 or 12. It takes a long time to learn how to throw well and to be able to pitch "strikes." After you have learned how to throw and want to practice pitching, draw a "strike zone" (about 17 inches wide by 24 inches tall) on the fence or the side of the house. With a tennis ball or a rubber ball, see how many times you can hit the strike zone from 45 feet away. Good Little League pitchers are able to hit the "strike zone" 6 out of 10 tries. Practicing this way is also good for learning how to catch the ball as it bounces back to you in the air or on the ground.

Pitching from the "Set" Position

It is a good idea to learn how to pitch, even if you never are called on to pitch. There are two positions that most Little League pitchers use. The "set" position is the easiest and best for boys who are just learning. In this position, right-handers stand with the sole of their right foot along the front edge of the pitcher's "rubber," which is in the middle of the pitcher's mound. Never try to pitch with your foot

BEGINNING THE STRIDE: As your throwing arm goes back, lift your forward foot.

on top of the rubber, as your foot will slip when you throw, making it hard for you to throw straight. You always "push" against the front edge of the rubber

CHEST TURN: As your arm sweeps up and also as you release the ball, your chest should be facing the batter.

with your right or "pivot foot." Your right foot may be on the ground in front of the rubber as long as the side of your shoe where your little toe rests is touching

THE DELIVERY: Your stride has ended and you let your arm sweep through.

FOLLOW-THROUGH: As your arm crosses your body, your right foot comes up, and you move into fielding position.

the rubber. Your left foot should lie 4 or 5 inches in front of your right foot and the toe of each shoe and your body must be turned toward third base. In this position, your left side, arm and shoulder will be turned toward the batter. You throw as you normally throw, by taking a short stride and "pivoting" or turning on your right foot and turning your chest toward the batter as you let go of the ball. (Left-handers of course push off with their left foot.)

Wind-Up Pitching Position

You can throw a much faster ball using the "wind-up" position, but you may not be able to throw as many strikes. In this position, if you are right-handed, start by placing your left foot behind the rubber 4 to 6 inches and your right foot on the rubber. The toes of your right foot may be "hooked" over the front edge and pointed toward the batter or a little toward third base. Or, you may stand on the rubber with both feet. You begin your wind-up by leaning forward a little with both arms down and in front of you. Hold the ball in your mitt with your right hand. Move your weight back on your left foot a little, bringing your hands (with ball and glove) above your head, and then pause a second or two. You complete your wind-up by bringing your right arm and hand behind your back with the ball behind you as you step or stride with your left foot toward the batter. As you step forward, you turn your body, your left shoulder and your left side toward the batter. You finish the throw as you would in the set position, turning your chest and body toward the batter. Keep your gloved hand in front of you ready to catch the ball if it is batted back to you.

Using a wind-up gives a pitcher a little more strength in throwing fast balls. It is also harder for the batter to hit the ball because the pitcher's arms, body and legs are all moving at once, and he has a hard time watching the ball.

START OF THE WIND-UP POSITION: Your feet can be on the rubber. Your body should be leaning forward, arms down in front of you.

SECOND STAGE OF WIND-UP: Weight goes back on your left foot, hands back too.

PEAK OF THE WIND-UP with hands above your head.

STARTING THE STRIDE: From wind-up over your head, you bring your pitching arm behind your back.

22 ◎ **Throwing**

DELIVERY from wind-up position: Your arm comes
forward and you follow through as in the photos on
pages 16 and 17, the same way as from the set position.

ANOTHER WAY TO START THE WIND-UP: The toe on the rubber will hook the front edge. The right foot will be used as a pivot.

STANCE FOR THE SET POSITION: The right little toe pressed up against the rubber is ready for the push-off.

The Fast Ball

All Little League ball players must know how to throw a fast ball. This is also the first pitch to learn and the best one to use most of the time. To throw a fast ball, hold or "grip" the ball as you would in throwing any ball. Your first and second fingers should be placed over two seams of the ball where they

FAST BALL GRIP: Front view shows the position of the thumb.

come close together, with the thumb also over a seam. (See illustration.) To make the throw, bring your arm back beyond your ear with your elbow bent. Then move forward, snapping your wrist downward just as the ball is released. Try to send it straight to the plate by pushing it off with your two fingers.

You need strength in your arms and shoulders to throw a good fast ball. This requires constant practice in throwing the ball. You might be able to make

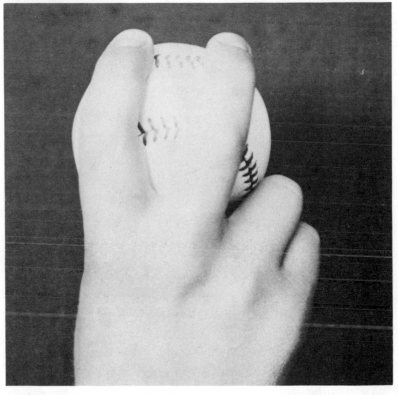

BASIC GRIP for throwing from fielding positions is the same as for a fast ball pitch. Note how the first and second fingers are over the seams at the narrow part.

LEFT-HANDER'S GRIP for a fast ball.

your shoulders and arms stronger by doing 15 to 20 push-ups and 5 to 8 pull-ups each day. At first you may not be able to do this many, but try to do as many as you can.

You should learn to let the ball go or "release" it

the same way each time. If you release it while your throwing arm and hand are above your head, you probably will throw the ball high. If you release it after your hand and arm have fallen below the level of your shoulder, you probably will throw the ball low. The best point is to release the ball somewhere in between. The exact point depends upon how tall you are, how strongly you can pitch, and how stiff your wrist is.

You have to try several different ways until you find the release point which is best for you. You might find, for example, that you can throw more strikes by bringing your arm straight over your shoulder and releasing the ball just a little ahead of your face. Or you might find that you can throw more strikes by bringing your arm a little farther away from your head and releasing the ball a little later. Finding out for yourself comes only with practice. After you find the best release point, practice until you can throw strikes.

After you have learned to throw the fast ball well, you can start to work with the "let-up" pitch, the sidearm pitch and finally the curve, but you must learn the fast ball first.

The "Let-Up" Pitch

This is nothing more than a fast ball thrown very slowly. The grip is the same and if you throw it right, the batter thinks you are throwing a fast ball. This

THE THREE-QUARTER OVERHAND PITCH is the natural way to throw a fast ball and a let-up pitch, or any pitch, for that matter.

fools him, and he will swing too soon. You use exactly the same movements, but instead of throwing the ball hard, you throw it easily . . . just hard enough to make it cross the plate. If you can throw it so that it starts out high, then drops through the strike zone, it is even better.

Many major league pitchers throw the "let-up" pitch (or "change of pace" as it is also called) by keeping their wrist stiff as they release the ball. Some 11- and 12-year-old pitchers get good enough to do this, but it takes a lot of practice. And it can only be done after you have mastered the fast ball. You can throw a let-up almost as well by just throwing easily, and not gripping the ball quite so hard.

Two things you must remember about the let-up pitch: First of all, never throw it to a batter who doesn't hit very well. A poor hitter usually can't hit fast balls, but he can hit a slowly-thrown ball such as a let-up pitch. The second thing to remember is that you must not throw it very often. It works only when it surprises the batter. Usually you throw it to a good hitter who is trying to hit a home run and has already missed two strikes. In this situation, he is expecting a fast ball, and will swing at the let-up pitch before the ball reaches the plate. He will miss by a mile and become very angry with himself!

The Sidearm Pitch

The sidearm pitch is thrown much like the fast ball. The only difference is that you keep your arm out at the side of your shoulder and body, instead of

SIDEARM PITCH: Keep your arm out at the side of your shoulder and body. Use it to fool the batter, but wait until you know how to throw a fast ball.

32 ◎ **Throwing**

above your head. The ball is released from your two fingers, just like the fast ball. All the other movements are the same also. Because the ball is released from your side, it surprises the hitter. It is more difficult to throw a strike with a sidearm pitch than with a fast ball. It takes constant practice, so don't try it until after you have learned how to throw a fast ball.

The Curve

A right-handed pitcher throws a curve directly at a right-handed batter. At the last moment, it turns or "curves" left and goes over the plate. The hitter thinks the ball will hit him or miss the plate on the inside, so he lets it go by.

Actually a curve is no harder to hit than any other pitch, if the batter knows the pitch is a curve and swings at it. If the batter is expecting a fast ball, and the pitcher throws a curve, it catches the hitter by surprise.

A curve is a good pitch to mix up with fast balls, sidearm pitches, and let-up pitches. It loses its value if a pitcher throws it all the time.

When a right-handed pitcher throws a curve to a left-handed hitter, he throws it wide of the plate. The idea is for it to curve "in" to the left-handed swinger and catch him by surprise. By the time the hitter decides it is a curve, it is too late for him to get a good swing at it.

A right-handed batter who stands close to the plate

OVERHAND PITCH: Your arm stays closer to your ear in this than in the three-quarter overhand. If you can control the ball and use the three different types of releases, your pitching will be more effective.

makes it harder for a right-handed pitcher to throw a curve into the strike zone. But if you pitch a curve directly at him, he will jump back as the ball curves into the strike zone. The main value of a curve is to keep the batter from getting set to hit a strike when you pitch it. You must keep the batter guessing. A good pitcher will alternate his pitches. Of course there are exceptions. For example, if a pitcher discovers that a batter cannot hit a curve he might throw nothing but curves.

The curve ball is hard to master. Boys who are big for their age can probably start throwing it by the time they are 10 years old, but usually boys should wait until aged 11 or 12 to work on it, as it is hard on your elbow and arm. Practicing it before you are old enough might hurt your arm and keep you from being a pitcher. Let your coach or your dad tell you when you are old enough to work on the curve ball.

The curve is thrown much like the fast ball. All the body movements are the same, and the pitching stance is the same. The four chief differences are: you hold or grip the ball differently. You turn your wrist so that the ball leaves your hand over the top of your first finger. Your second finger gives the ball the spin, and the release point may be different. Let's look at these differences a little closer.

THE CURVE GRIP: Hold the ball with your second finger running along a seam or stitch on the ball.

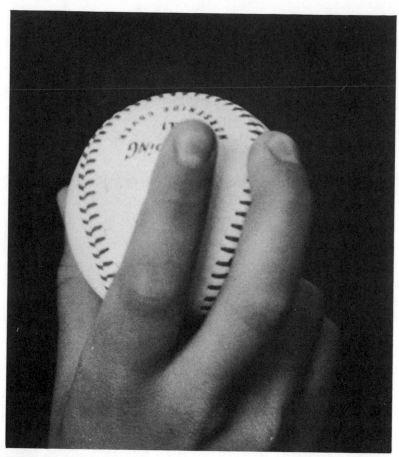

CURVE BALL GRIP: A special grip for Little League ball players. See how the second finger is held along the seam.

Place your first finger between two seams or stitches. The ball must slide over your first or top finger while your second or bottom finger (the one on the seam) gives it the spin.

TURNING YOUR WRIST: In throwing a fast ball, you snap your wrist downward. With a curve ball, you turn your wrist. The ball must be released from your hand by rolling over your first or top finger.

GIVING THE BALL SPIN: For a curve, you need to place the full length of your second finger along a seam. Take a tight grip on the ball. As you release the

CURVE BALL ABOUT TO BE RELEASED: Your wrist has to turn over as you deliver. The ball goes out over the top of your fingers.

PITCHING PRACTICE SCHEDULE

Boys should practice at least 10 to 15 minutes each day.
Always start by "warming up" for 2 to 3 minutes using easy pitches.

AGE	Throwing Catching	Fast Ball	"Let-Up"	Sidearm	Curve Ball	"Knuckle" Ball
6–9	Start with rubber or tennis ball. Use baseball when you can throw and catch a rubber or tennis ball well. Always use a mitt and work on correct position.	Practice each day after you can throw and catch a baseball well.	Don't practice this very much. Wait until you are 10.	Forget about this until you can throw a "fast" ball.	Forget about this until you are 11.	Don't work with this until you are 11.
9	Continue to develop good form. Practice each day with baseball and mitt.	Practice each day with some-one. You might make yourself a target of bailed hay or use a "pitch-back" or something. Work on accuracy and speed.				
10			Work on this as you gain confidence and accuracy.			
11				*After* you can throw a good "fast" ball, practice this from different positions.	Start experimenting until you can get the ball to "break" then work hard on it.	Experiment with different grips until you can throw the ball without much spin.
12	*Practice every day!*	*Practice every day!*	*Practice every day!*	*Practice every day!*	*Practice every day!*	*Practice every day!*

Work to improve your form and concentrate on a "fast" ball and "curve" ball. Use the other pitches if you can make them work for you. Try to pitch at least 5 strikes of every 10 balls you throw.

ball, it goes over your top finger, and your second finger pulls against the seam to give the ball spin.

THE RELEASE POINT: Releasing the fast ball from different positions makes it high or low as it crosses the plate. Releasing the curve ball from different positions also makes it do different things. If you use a sidearm pitch but throw it as a curve, the ball will curve and also drop a little.

Most boys find it hard to aim the curve ball. With a fast ball, you aim it right over the plate. If you are a good pitcher, it will usually go over the plate. Right-handed pitchers with a curve ball should aim just a little to the right of the plate (3 to 4 inches). Then, when the curve "breaks," it goes over the plate. This is the reason you see so many right-handed hitters jumping back from the plate—the pitcher tries to throw a curve (aiming it just a little "inside"). When it doesn't break or curve as it should, it hits the batter unless he jumps back.

The "Knuckle" Ball

This is also a hard pitch for Little Leaguers to learn. With this pitch, the ball moves through the air with little or no spin. It surprises the hitter. If he does get a good swing at it, chances are he'll pop it up rather than get a good hit. You throw it with the same movement as the fast ball, but with a different grip. Big leaguers grip the ball with their knuckles, rather than with their fingers. Boys whose hands are

KNUCKLE BALL: Most boys find it easier to throw this pitch by gripping the ball with their fingers and not their knuckles. It is not a good pitch for young players.

not big enough can throw this by gripping the ball with the tips of their fingers rather than with their knuckles. As the ball leaves the hand, it "slides" rather than spins.

It is not a very good pitch for Little Leaguers to use. The let-up pitch is just as good, and is not as hard to master.

HITTING

Hitting is the heart of baseball. Winning teams usually win because their players can hit the ball. Almost every baseball game is won or lost because of the way the team's players hit. A Little League team was behind one run in the ninth inning when the boy at bat got the first home run he ever hit, winning the ball game by one run. His team won because he was able to hit the ball. If you can't hit, you can't help your team much and you won't enjoy the game very much.

Your great pleasure will come when you feel the bat hitting the ball. You'll be happiest when you hear the "crack" of the bat as it sends the ball way out into the field or over the fence. You will not be happy to strike out all the time. You want to be a good hitter? You are willing to learn how to hit? Here's how you can do it.

Choose the Right Bat

Good hitting starts with the bat. You have to find one that is right for you and then use it right. Little League bats come in different lengths. The shortest

BAT NUMBERS: The shortest is 27 inches long (stamped 7) and the largest for Little League is 32 (stamped 2).

bat is 27 inches long, and the longest bat is 32 inches long. These lengths are stamped on the end of the handle, with just the last number. For example: a 27-inch bat is stamped with a "7" and a 32-inch bat is stamped with a "2".

Most boys make the mistake of thinking they can hit better with a longer bat. This is not always the case. As a general rule, the older and larger boys should use the longest bats, and the younger and smaller boys should use the shorter bats. The shorter the bat, the faster you can swing. The important thing to remember is to use a bat you can swing easily. If the bat is too long and too heavy for you, you will not be able to get good hits.

Each bat has a "label" (the brand name of the company which makes it) stamped in a special place. Some ball players believe that if this label is not on top, the bat will break if the ball hits that spot. This is not true, say the bat makers, so hold it as your coach tells you.

HITTING AREA: Aim your bat to hit the ball between the two black marks and you will get a good hit. If the ball hits above or below the marks you will not get a good hit.

GRIP the bat with the knuckles of your hands lined up, as shown here. This batter is choking up on the bat about 3 inches. He is probably facing a fast pitcher or is trying to place the ball in left field.

Grip the Bat Right

As you pick up and grip a bat, notice where your knuckles are. The second knuckle of your lower hand should be lined up between the first and second knuckles of your top hand. Try it. You'll find that it feels good. If your knuckles are in any other position, it will not feel as good to you when you swing the bat in hitting.

GRIP THE BAT TIGHTLY. If you hold it loosely, it will sting your hands when you hit the ball. In cold weather it will sting more than in hot weather. If you have early morning practices you will find that most of the bats will sting because they are cold. If the ball comes too close to your hands when your bat hits it, that will also cause a sting. If you hold the bat tightly, it will not sting quite so much.

"CHOKE" THE BAT. In baseball, "choke" means to move your hands a little way up the bat. Many good hitters place their bottom hand about 2 inches above the end of the bat. This helps them swing faster. It is good advice always to choke up a little even if you are using a 27-inch bat. When carpenters use a hammer, they always choke up a little . . . it gives them a faster swing and better aim. The same thing is true in baseball. If the pitcher is throwing very

NEVER BAT WITHOUT A HELMET: Made of tough plastic and lined with soft rubber, the helmet protects you at bat and while base running.

PROPER BAT POSITION: His front elbow should be a little higher, but otherwise this is fine.

fast balls, try choking up more on your bat; it will help you to swing faster.

Bat Position

Keep the bat away from your body. As you wait in the batter's box for the pitcher to throw the ball, hold the bat a little away from your body . . . about 3 to 6 inches should be enough. This helps you to swing at most pitches. If you held your bat close to your body and the pitcher threw the ball a little on the "inside" (close to your body), you would not hit the ball with the fat part of the bat. You would hit it near your hands. And if the pitcher came in on the "outside" of the plate, you would not be able to reach the ball. If you hold the bat a short distance away from the body, you will be able to get a better swing at every pitch.

Hold your hands above your rear foot and even with your chest. In this position, your bat is ready for action. It is far enough back and high enough that you can start swinging quickly. You will notice some boys trying to hold their bat way behind their backs. In this position they have a hard time swinging around in time to hit the ball, and most of the time they miss it. Holding the bat in this way, the proper way—above your rear foot and level with your chest— you can swing at most balls: the high ones, the low ones, the "outside" ones or the "inside" ones.

Your front elbow should be even with your hands.

LINING UP: As you take your place in the batter's box, make certain that you can cover the entire width of the plate with your bat.

If you raise your front elbow too high, your arm and shoulder will hide the pitcher, and you can't watch the ball. If your front elbow is too low, you might swing under the ball. The best way is to hold your front elbow even (on a level) with your hands holding the bat.

In the Batter's Box

When you are in the batter's box, you have to be ready to swing at each ball that the pitcher throws. This may not seem to be very important, but it is one of the first things you need to learn if you are to be a good hitter.

You must believe that you can hit the ball. If you don't think you can hit the ball, the chances are that you won't hit it. When one of your teammates is in the batter's box, you must help him to get ready by telling him he can hit the ball. Let him know that you believe he can hit it.

YOU MUST WANT TO HIT. Some boys get in the batter's box and hope the pitcher will walk him. There are boys who would rather be walked than hit the ball. You can't be a good hitter if you think this way. Hope the pitcher throws you a good pitch so you can get a good swing at it.

DON'T LET THE PITCHER FOOL YOU. Sometimes the pitcher will stand on the rubber a long time before throwing the ball. He does this to get your mind off the game and to start you thinking about something else. Before you can get your mind back on the ball game, he can strike you out. If the pitcher takes too long, step out of the batter's box for a few seconds. Then when *you* are ready, step back in the batter's box and wait for the pitch. The important thing to remember is that you must think about the ball the pitcher is going to throw and not about something else.

PICK OUT THE GOOD BALLS. You must first learn where your strike zone is and then swing only at those balls which come through it. Your strike zone is

BATTING STANCE: Probably the best place to stand is in the middle of the box, with your rear foot a little farther back from the plate.

between your knees and your shoulders and is the width of home plate—18 inches wide and about 30 inches high. Ted Williams was a great hitter because he never swung at bad pitches. The strike zone he called his "Happy Zone" and he knew exactly where the ball had to be in order for him to get a good hit. Don't swing at balls which are not in your strike zone. In other words, learn the difference between strikes and balls.

"KEEP YOUR EYE ON THE BALL." You frequently hear the coaches yell this at hitters. Do you know what this means? Many boys don't. It means that you should keep watching the ball from the time the pitcher gets it until you see it hit your bat. Try to find the ball as he gets it and then watch it closely— even during his wind-up. Watch it as it leaves his hand and as it comes toward the batter's box. Good hitters say they watch the ball as it hits their bat, and they can see this happening. You can't hit the ball with your eyes shut. You can't hit the ball if you are looking at the pitcher or the place you think you are going to knock the ball. You have to "keep your eye on the ball."

Stance

The batter's box for Little League boys is 36 inches by 66 inches. Both feet must be in the batter's box when you hit the ball. If one of your feet is outside of the line when you hit the ball, the umpire will call

WRONG POSITION: This batter would be called out as he hits the ball because one foot is outside the batter's box. He should stand farther back, so his stride doesn't take him too far forward.

you "out" even if you hit a home run. If the pitcher is throwing fast balls, some boys like to stand at the rear of the batter's box. This gives them more time to watch the ball. If the pitcher is throwing lots of curve balls, some boys like to stand in the front of the box to hit the ball before it "breaks" or curves. The only trouble with these ideas is that you don't know what kind of a ball the pitcher is going to throw, and you might be in the wrong place. Also, if you are standing in the front of the box, you might step forward and out of the box as you swing, and get called "out" even if you hit the ball. The best advice for Little League boys is to stand in the middle of the box with your toes just 2 or 3 inches from the line that is near the plate.

How you stand in the box is just as important as where you stand.

BEND YOUR BACK AND KNEES A LITTLE. You have to be ready to move if the pitcher throws you a wild pitch. If you stand with both knees stiff, you will not be able to move quickly. On the other hand, if you bend your knees too much, you will look like you are ready to sit in a chair. You won't be able to hit as well either. If you don't bend your back a little, you can't move your arms easily. If you bend over too much, your head, arms and hands will be right over the plate, and the pitcher will hit you when he throws the ball over the plate. Experiment with this a little: Stand up straight, with your knees "locked" or stiff. Now

WAITING FOR A FAST PITCH: The batter's rear foot is far back in the box, near the line. His knees are slightly bent, and his feet about 12 inches apart. His stance is perfectly proper to hit a fast ball.

try to jump. Try it with your back straight and stiff too. It's hard to jump this way, isn't it? So we say: "Bend your back and knees a little."

STAND WITH YOUR FEET APART. Your back foot should be about 12 inches behind. You may notice some boys standing on their back foot with their front foot raised on their toes. This is not good. Your feet should be level about 12 inches apart. This places the weight of your body equally on each foot and helps you move all parts of your body to get more power into your swing. Boys who stand on one foot cannot get all their power into the swing. Your back foot should also be just an inch or two more back from the plate than the front foot. This also gives you a little more power and helps make your swing faster.

Point your front shoulder and hip toward the pitcher. As you stand in the batter's box, your whole side should point toward the pitcher. This gives you full power in your swing. If you start your swing by standing in the box with your stomach aimed at the pitcher, your swing would make use of your arm muscles alone. Standing with your side aimed at the pitcher helps you use your back and shoulder muscles as well as your arm muscles and this gives you much more power.

Swinging the Bat

When you swing, or, as we say in baseball, when you "cut" at the ball, you must make all your muscles

TAKE A SHORT STEP: This batter has taken too long a stride. His helmet has fallen over his eyes, and he can't see the ball, which has probably gone foul. Don't try to "murder" the ball.

work together so that the bat hits the ball. Although everything has to be done together, we can look at parts of the swing and see what should take place when you swing.

TAKE A SHORT STEP. Your back foot stays in one place while your front foot moves toward the pitcher about 4 to 6 inches. You must not take a big step or it will make you swing under the ball. It will also make you move your eyes. Have you ever stepped off a step in the dark? Remember how it hurt your neck and shook up your head? The same thing happens when you take a big step in hitting . . . it shakes your head so that you can't see the ball very well.

You can't hit well if you don't take a step, because you won't get all your back and shoulder muscles working. But taking a big step might make you miss the ball. Also, if you take a big step, you might step right out of the batter's box.

Take your step toward the pitcher and not toward third or first base. Right-handed hitters sometimes step toward third base, which takes some of the power out of their swing and aims the ball over third base. The same thing happens to left-handed hitters as they step and hit toward first base. In baseball we say they are "stepping in the bucket" when they do this. So, to be a good hitter, take a small step toward the pitcher as you start your swing or cut.

TURN TOWARD THE PITCHER. Try swinging without turning your hips. You'll see that this is hard to do and hurts a little. You can't swing easily unless you also turn your body. When you do it properly, your stomach should be pointing right at the pitcher as your bat hits the ball.

PUSH WITH YOUR BACK FOOT. You do this when you take a step. As you push, your front leg is straight

PUSH WITH YOUR BACK FOOT: As you step forward, you will get more power in your swing this way. This batter is going for a knee-high pitch, but swinging level with the ball.

and you put your weight into the swing, getting all the power you can from your arms, back and shoulders. You must remember to have both feet on the ground when your bat hits the ball. If you hit the ball while you are taking the step, your front foot will be off the ground, robbing you of power. If you lift your back foot off the ground, you will also lose

KEEP YOUR HEAD STEADY: This left-handed batter is watching the ball. As he swings, he keeps his front leg stiff after he has taken a short stride.

power. Having one or both feet off the ground as you swing will also make it hard for you to aim your bat at the ball, and you will miss the ball a lot.

KEEP YOUR SHOULDERS LEVEL. If you lower your front shoulder as you start your swing, it makes you swing under the ball. If you raise your front shoulder as you swing, you might swing over the ball.

SWING AT THE "TOP HALF" OF THE BALL. If you can

FOLLOW THROUGH: Don't halt your swing as you hit. Turn so that your belt buckle faces the pitcher and you keep looking ahead, with your shoulders level.

60 ◎ **Hitting**

do this, you can become a good hitter. Boys who try to swing up on the ball, hitting the bottom half of it, usually knock fly balls to the infield—and pop out.

KEEP YOUR HEAD STEADY. Sometimes hitters turn their head as they swing. When they do this, they can't watch the ball. A right-handed hitter who is trying to knock the ball over the left field fence will miss the ball if he turns his head and looks at the fence as he completes his swing. You should be looking at the ball as your bat hits it. Your back and shoulders turn, but your head doesn't.

AIM THE BAT AT THE BALL. The best place on the bat to hit the ball is just beyond the label. If you can aim your bat so that the ball hits it between the label and the top of the bat (not too near the tip), you will get good hits regularly.

FOLLOW-THROUGH. "Follow-through" is a word which is used in all sports. If you stop your swing just as the bat hits the ball, the ball won't go very far. Try stopping your practice swing right in the middle. You lose your power and you have a hard time aiming the bat. Your swing has to go all the way around. You must keep both hands on the bat without moving them. To do this, your wrists must turn. Your top arm must roll over your bottom arm after you hit the ball. If you twist your wrist and arms before you hit the ball, you won't get a good hit.

A GOOD BUNT: See how the ball drops dead.

Bunting

A good bunt in baseball makes the ball roll a few feet into the infield, in front of the plate, either toward first base or third base. If there is a runner on third base, you might bunt the ball a few feet toward first base. Then, while the pitcher or first baseman is getting it, the runner from third could score. If you see that the third baseman is playing too near the shortstop, bunt the ball toward third base and you might get to first safely. There are many times when a good bunt will work well in a ball game. But bunting is not easy and you will need to practice a lot to be able to lay down a good bunt. Here is how you do it.

TAKE YOUR NORMAL STANCE. A bunt doesn't work very well if the other team knows you are going to bunt, so you must not let them know until the last minute. You start by standing in the batter's box just as if you were going to swing away at the ball. The only difference is that you stand just a little further away from the plate.

FACE THE PITCHER. As the pitcher throws the ball, you turn your stomach and feet toward the pitcher by moving your feet so that both toes are pointed toward him, with your back foot placed near the plate, but still in the batter's box.

HOLD THE BAT IN FRONT OF YOUR CHEST. Move your top hand along the bat to the label area with your fingers doubled up. The bat just rests between

BAT POSITION FOR BUNTING: Square around and face the pitcher at the last moment. Then just push the bat into the ball. Try to make it roll dead where the pitcher, catcher and basemen will have a hard time getting to it.

your fingers and thumb. You can't put your fingers all the way around the bat, or they might get hit by the ball. Hide them as much as you can behind the bat.

PUSH THE BAT TOWARD THE BALL. The bunt really is just a *push*, rather than a *swing* of the bat. Try to have the hitting area of the bat just meet the ball. The bat should only travel 4 to 6 inches. You don't want to hit the ball hard. Just push the ball, aiming it where you want it to go.

Practice

You can't be a good hitter unless you practice. For the best kind of practice, you need someone to throw the balls to you and you need someone to chase them. You can get your friends together and go to the vacant lot, the school grounds, the park or some place else and take turns hitting. If you can't do this, here are the other ways you can practice:

"PEPPER." Stand with your back near a fence or wall and have one or two of your friends line up about 20 feet away. Give each of them a turn tossing the ball to you while you try to hit the ball back to them. If you miss it, the boy on the end of the line takes your place. If a boy misses fielding the ball as you hit it to him, he goes to the end of the line. This practice needs very little space. You can play it in your back yard, but you must not hit or throw the ball very hard. You might try bunting the ball rather than swinging at it. This would also give you good practice at bunting.

SWINGING AT "MAKE BELIEVE BALLS." If you are all alone, you can still practice hitting by just swinging the bat and playing that you are swinging at a ball. A door knob, a knothole in the fence, a rock on the ground can be the ball. You don't hit it with the bat, you just pretend that you do. Although it doesn't move, you pretend that it does. You try to aim your swing to hit it, as if it were a ball coming right at you.

HITTING "T": Make this from an old rubber hose and a broom handle. The hose has to be large enough to slide up and down, so it can be adjusted to give you practice hitting high and low "pitches." Place the "T" in front of the plate so that you get in the habit of hitting the ball as it crosses the plate.

This practice will help develop your wrists and arms and other muscles you use in hitting.

HITTING "T". You can make a hitting "T" with

an old broom handle about 20 inches long, and a piece of rubber hose 6 to 8 inches long. The rubber hose should be large enough to fit tight on the broom handle. Drive the broom handle into the ground and place the rubber hose on top of it. Then place a baseball on top of the rubber hose and swing at it with a bat. The hose can be adjusted up and down on the broom handle for your strike zone. The rubber hose is needed so that you won't ruin your bat or knock the broom stick out of the ground if you swing under the ball. You can work with other boys and play "broom stick derby" by seeing how far you can bat the ball. This will give you practice watching the ball and also strengthen the muscles you use in hitting.

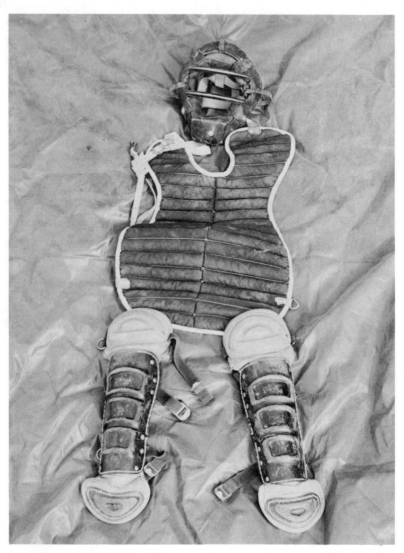

CATCHER'S GEAR: The mask protects your head, the chest protector covers chest and stomach, and the shin guards protect your lower legs.

THE CATCHER

A team must have good pitchers to win. But good teams must also have a good catcher. Pitchers could not be good pitchers if they didn't have a good catcher. In addition to knowing how to catch, the catcher must also be the "quarterback" or "field general" for the baseball team. You see, to be a good catcher, you must really know baseball.

The catcher is the only man on the team who can see the whole field and all the players at once. When a "heavy" hitter comes to the plate, it is the catcher who should make sure the outfielders are in the right place. He has to check before each pitch to make sure that all the players are in the right places. If they are not in the right position, he should hold the game up by calling "time out" until they move to the right places. If the next hitter is a left-handed hitter, the catcher should make sure that the infielders and outfielders have shifted toward right field and toward first base. Most left-handed batters hit the ball to the right of second base. The catcher must know when to move the outfield toward the fence, and when to pull them in closer to the infield.

SIGNALING: Two fingers down may call for a curve. One finger might be a fast ball and three fingers might be a let-up pitch. If the pitcher doesn't agree with the catcher's call, he shakes off the signal and gets another.

Working with the Pitcher

The catcher must work very closely with the pitcher. He must know what kind of a pitch is coming, and hold his mitt in the right place so the pitcher can use it as a target. For this reason, pitchers and catchers usually work with signals. The catcher has to give the signals, because everybody in the ball park could "read" the signals if the pitcher gave them. So the catcher tells the pitcher what kind of a pitch he thinks would work best. If the pitcher doesn't want to throw that pitch he says "no" to the catcher by shaking his head side to side. The catcher gives a signal for another pitch. Sometimes the catcher has to call "time out" and walk out to talk to the pitcher. He must make sure he knows that the next pitch will be.

The catcher gives the signals by holding his fingers between his legs while he is in the catching position. This hides the signals from the other team. One finger might mean a fast ball. Two fingers might mean a curve. Three fingers might mean a let-up pitch. The important thing to remember is that if a battery (catcher and pitcher) is using signals, make sure that both of you know what they are. Even the infield ought to be able to read the signals.

Catcher's Equipment

You must wear the right equipment if you are going to catch. All of it has been made to help keep you from getting hurt. The leg protectors are made to

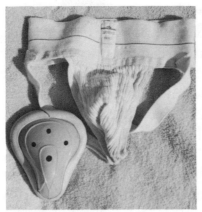
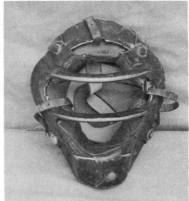

THE CUP (left) is a much-needed protection for a catcher to wear under an athletic supporter. The MASK (right), padded on the inside is held on by strong straps which are easily stretched so that you can remove the mask fast when chasing foul flies and wild pitches.

CHEST GUARDS (left) are made of soft material. Notice that the left shoulder is larger than the right to allow you to throw easier with your right arm. SHIN GUARDS (right) protect ankles and knees as well as shins.

cover your lower legs and knees. When you are in place and ready to catch, the upper parts of your legs will not get hit by the ball, but your knees, shins and ankles may—and they must be covered. The protectors must fit you well, so they won't be sliding off.

Your chest must also be protected, so make sure that you wear the chest protector, and that it fits you. The face mask protects your face and it must fit well, but you must also be able to get it off fast to catch fly balls, and to make plays at the plate.

Almost everyone knows about the leg guards, the chest protector, and the face guard, because they see them in every baseball game, but very few people know about the "cup," because it is seldom seen. This is made of metal or plastic and is worn inside your pants, in front, and under your underwear or athletic supporter. An athletic supporter protects you, and ought to be worn by everybody who plays baseball. A cup, worn under your athletic supporter, protects you still more, especially if you get hit between the legs with a ball, bat, foot or leg.

The catcher's glove or mitt, of course, is made to protect your hands and fingers from foul balls, and swinging bats, as well as to help you catch the ball. All this equipment should be worn each time you get behind the plate to catch . . . even in practice.

Be Quick

Catchers must be able to move quickly. If the

SQUAT POSITION: Stay about an arm's length away from the batter. Squat between pitches to save your energy. Use your mitt as a target for the pitcher.

pitcher lets a wild pitch loose, the catcher must move quickly to get it, or it might allow a run to score. The catcher can usually set the pace of the game. If he is slow and acts as if he doesn't care whether he wins or loses, the rest of the team will act the same. If the catcher is lively, and shows plenty of team spirit, the team will also be lively and full of team spirit. In baseball language, we say the catcher must have lots of "hustle." This means he is always working fast and hard to do his job right. When a hitter pops the ball in the air around the plate, the catcher must take off his mask quickly so he can see the ball, and get under it fast. If he just stands there and lets it drop, the team knows he isn't doing his best. You have to be quick, and you have to be fast, and your legs must be strong if you want to be a good catcher.

A Good Throwing Arm

Catchers must have a good throwing arm. You must be able to throw the ball hard and fast to second base. If a team thinks the catcher doesn't have a good throwing arm, they will try to steal second all the time. A catcher who has to throw the ball high in order to get it to second base takes too much time in throwing. The runner will get there before the ball. How many times have you seen a catcher try to throw to second base and miss? If the ball gets away from the second baseman, and goes clear out into the outfield, the runner will go to third and, in some cases, all the way to home. To be a good catcher you have to practice throwing a low, fast ball to second base. Aim for the knees of the baseman so that he can make a good tag when he gets the ball.

The Right Way to Catch

People can tell if you are a good catcher by watching how you "sit" behind the plate . . . waiting for the pitcher to throw the ball. These tips might help:

LOW PITCH: At all costs, the catcher must prevent the ball from getting through his legs. Here he has caught the bad pitch in his glove. Another way to stop the ball is to turn your mitt over and trap the ball against the ground (see page 80).

STAY ABOUT AN ARM'S LENGTH FROM THE HITTER. If you get closer, the batter might hit you as he swings, or he might "throw" the bat after he swings and hit you. You must not be so close that his bat will hit you or your glove. If this happens, it is like being hit by the pitcher: the hitter gets a free walk to first base.

LET YOUR MITT BE THE TARGET. Get straight behind the plate, and make your body the strike zone for the pitcher. Hold your glove still, so the pitcher can use it for a target. Find out where he likes to have you hold your mitt for each pitch he wants to use. Then hold it still.

DON'T MOVE TOWARD THE BALL. Let the ball come to you. Stay in your place, and hold your glove still for the pitcher. Be ready to move to either side, up or down, but don't move into the batter's box to catch the ball.

KNEEL OR SQUAT BETWEEN PITCHES. Check to see if the players are in the right places before you give the signal to the pitcher. Squatting doesn't take much of your strength, and it gives you a little rest between action. Of course if there are men on the bases, you can't do this—you would need to be ready for action.

KEEP YOUR EYES OPEN. Keep your head straight ahead. Many boys cannot catch well because they shut their eyes as the hitter swings at the ball. When you do this, you can't see the ball! If the batter misses

"CHAIR POSITION": The catcher looks as if he is about ready to sit in a chair. This is the position most catchers like best. Notice how his knees are better protected than in the squat position. By keeping his right hand behind his mitt, he avoids injury to his bare fingers. Another way would be to double up his fingers in a fist, or turn his palm toward himself.

the ball, or fouls it back to you, it is impossible for you to see and catch it. Don't turn your head. The mask is made to protect your face, but it will not protect the side of your head. If the ball hits you on the ear, it will hurt.

"Chair Position"

Make believe you are ready to sit in a chair when the pitcher throws the ball. The right catcher's position is just that. Stay behind the hitter. Make believe that someone is pulling the chair out from under you, keeping yourself from falling of course. Take this position just as the pitcher is ready to pitch, and you would be in almost the right catching form.

Some catchers try to catch while kneeling on one or both knees. The upper parts of their legs are not protected this way, and their legs could get hurt with the ball. Also, in this position, they can't get up fast enough to make good throws. Some catchers also try to catch by sitting on their heels. Sitting like this, a ball could hit them between the legs and hurt them.

When you are in the chair position, your body is upright, but leaning forward a little. Because you bend at the hips, your legs look as if someone could slide a chair under you. If the pitch is low, high, inside or outside, you can move quickly to get it. You are also ready to make a throw as you catch the ball. A catcher who kneels or squats has a hard time catching wild pitches, and is likely to be slow making throws.

TRAPPING THE PITCH IN THE DIRT: To make sure you block the ball, turn your mitt pocket down and press it against the ground.

Try it for yourself. If you kneel, you can't get going fast enough to reach a wild pitch or make a good throw. Try doing it right. It is harder, but you can really get moving fast. It will take you a while for your legs to become strong enough to catch this way, but it is the best.

Your Throwing Hand

Most catchers get hurt because they don't know how to hide their throwing hand, and it gets hit by a foul ball. Some catchers like to place their throwing hand on the back of their mitt, letting the glove hide it. Some like to double up the fingers of their throwing hand, then open them after the ball gets into the mitt. Some major league catchers say the safest and best way is to turn the back of their throwing hand toward the pitcher. They keep it behind the mitt. Then, if the ball hits the fingers of your hand held in this position, your fingers will bend. If your hand is held the opposite way, with the palm facing the pitcher, your fingers would bend backwards if the ball hits them, and they would be broken or badly hurt.

Catching Fly Balls

When the batter hits a high fly ball straight up in the air—over the batter's box, to the right or left of it (part way to first or third), or behind it—the catcher should try to get it. If it is going toward the pitcher, let the third baseman or first baseman have it. It is much easier for a player to catch a high fly ball when it is moving toward him.

The catcher's hardest job is to catch a twisting fly.

The first thing you as a catcher must do is find out where a fly is—to the right, to the left, straight up? Then you throw your mask in the opposite direction, so you won't trip on it. You can't see well enough

FORCE PLAY AT HOME: You can stand up tall in front of the plate, and step back to touch the plate when the ball hits your mitt. Be ready to throw if another runner is on base.

when you keep your mask on while trying to catch a fly ball. Get under the fly as fast as you can and wait for it. In using a catcher's glove, it might be easier to catch the ball by holding the mitt, pocket side up, about even with your chest. Use your free hand to cover the mitt and ball as the ball hits the pocket. If you don't cover it, it might spin or jump out of the glove.

Dropping the Mask

The mask lets you see well straight ahead, as you watch the ball being thrown by the pitcher. But it is hard to see well to the side or straight up with the mask on. So you have to take it off when you catch fly balls. You also should take it off when you have to catch the ball to make a tag at the plate. There are times when you won't have time, but if you have time, get rid of the mask fast. Throw it out of the way, where it won't trip or hurt anyone. Don't drop it on the plate or in the batter's box. Don't throw it toward the infield. Throw it toward the stands or screen.

Making the Tag at the Plate

The catcher has to be ready for a runner trying to steal home. Also a catcher often has a chance to tag out a runner trying to score on a base hit. You must learn to tag a runner without hurting him or yourself.

Some catchers in the major leagues try to get between the runner and home plate. This might

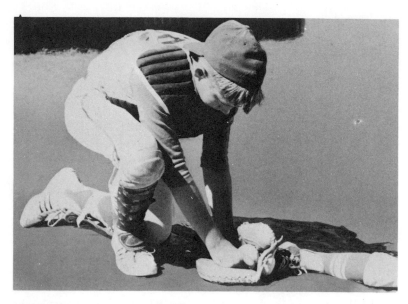

Hold the ball in your mitt and let the runner slide into it.

The runner is coming in from outside the foul line.

THREE PLAYS AT THE PLATE: (Above) The ball has gone past the catcher. He has chased it and will throw it to the pitcher, covering the plate. But the pitcher is in danger. The runner may slide into his right leg and also he might jar the ball loose. The pitcher should have his feet in the position of the catcher in the photo on the bottom of the opposite page, but with his side turned left. Then the runner, if he slides, will not hit him or touch the plate without touching his glove (with the ball, hopefully). In the picture at the top of the opposite page, the catcher has had time to take the throw and get down on one knee so as not to get knocked over by the sliding runner.

succeed in getting the runner out, but it also might hurt the catcher or the runner. The best and safest way is to stand on the inside side, right in front of the plate while you catch the ball. Turn to your left when you have the ball, and tag or wait for the runner. Tag him with your bare hand—holding the ball tightly—or hold it in your mitt with your bare hand so it won't get knocked out. Make the tag just "brushing" him with the back of your mitt when you have the ball in it.

If the runner slides, turn to your left, and kneel down with the ball held tightly in your mitt. Turn the back of the glove toward the runner, and let him slide into the mitt as he comes toward the plate. Be sure to tag low so he won't slide under your tag.

If it is a force play, stand in front of the plate, just as when you are going to make a tag on a runner. When you catch the ball, step back with your right foot, and tag the plate with your heel. Doing it this way, you are ready to make a throw to one of the other bases for a double play. If there is no chance for a double play, you are out of the way of the runner. If you stand right on top of the plate, he may knock you over as he runs by, or step on your foot.

Covering the Bases

A catcher must be ready to back up (or "cover") first and third bases. On batted balls, with no runners on base, the catcher should always run down the first base line so he can stop or run after the ball if the first baseman misses it. Don't do this if there are runners on base, especially on second or third base, as they might score while you are down by first base. If the third baseman fields a bunt with a runner on first base only, the catcher should run toward third to cover it to keep the runner from going to third.

Bunts

Bunts down the third base line should be handled by the third baseman or, in some cases, by the pitcher. Bunts in front of the plate, or half-way to first base or to the pitcher, should be handled by the catcher. It is best to use both hands. Use your mitt to stop or smother the ball, and your throwing hand to scoop it up and throw it. If the ball stops, and is not moving, pick it up with your throwing hand.

CLEATS: These shoes are the best for base running. The shoe on the left has rubber cleats, soccer type. The shoe on the right also has rubber cleats, baseball type. Metal-spiked shoes are not used by Little Leaguers.

RUNNING THE BASES

When you get a good hit, how do you get to first base? Sounds like a silly question, doesn't it? But do you know that you can be called "out" for not running to first base in the right way? Do you know that you can also be called "out" on a home run? If you are on first or second base and try to steal the next base, do you know you can be called "out"? You can be the best hitter on the team, but if you don't know how to run the bases, you might as well stay in the dugout.

Reaching First Base

If you will look closely the next time you are at the ball park, you will notice two white lines drawn on the field between home plate and first base. One of the lines (the foul line) goes from the plate through first base and to the outfield. The other line starts about half-way from the plate and runs to first base about 18 inches away from the foul line. When you are running from the plate to first base, you have to run

RUNNING OUT A SINGLE: This runner is approaching first base correctly, and will run to the outside of the bag after he tags it. Notice that he is running to the outside of the foul line, along a thinner chalk line which indicates the edge of the base path. He should tag the outside corner of the bag with his left foot as he crosses it. The first baseman is taking a nice long stretch toward the ball, while tagging the inside corner of the bag. Neither boy will get hurt on this play. If the runner thinks he will be able to get more than a single on his hit, he will approach first base differently, as in the photo on page 92.

on the outside of the foul line all the way and between the two lines as you come near to first base.

There is a reason for this. Let's say you bunt in front of the plate. The catcher has to throw you out at first base. If the ball thrown by the catcher touches you while you are inside the first white line (the foul line), you will be "out." This is called "interference," and the umpire has to call you "out." If you get in the way of the first baseman, making him miss the ball, it is also "interference." Although in this case, the ball doesn't hit you, you will be called "out."

This is one of the "fairness" rules in baseball. It would not be fair for one of the infielders to trip or push you down while you are trying to run to first base. And it would not be fair for you to wave your arms and cap, or get in front of the first baseman so he couldn't catch the ball. You should have a fair chance to get to first base, and the first baseman must have a fair chance to get you out. So when you are running to first base, keep between the two white lines as you come near the bag.

Another thing to remember about first base is that you should step on the outside corner of the bag. If the first baseman is playing the bag as he should, he would be tagging the inside corner of the bag, and giving you the outside corner. This will help keep both boys from getting hurt. If you both stepped on the top of the bag at the same time, can you guess what would happen? One of you would get your foot

RUNNING OUT AN EXTRA-BASE HIT: This is the correct way to touch first base when you have hit a possible double, triple or home run. You come across the base with your right foot tagging the inside corner of the bag. You lean toward the inside to take a short-cut to second base.

stepped on, and you might trip each other. So, tag the *outside* corner of the bag with your left foot, if possible, and turn toward the fence . . . away from the playing field. If you turn into the playing field, you might be tagged out even though you reached first base safely. The other team, and the umpire, would think you were trying to go on to second base. If you get a good hit and think you can make it to second base, tag the *inside* corner of the base with your *right* foot and go on to second base as fast as you can. The coach behind first base will wave his arm and call to you: "Go for two" if he thinks you can make it.

Another thing you should do when running to first base is make sure you run! Run without looking to see where the ball has gone. Run hard even if you hit a fly ball or a grounder that looks like a sure out. The fielder might miss it or fumble it. If you stopped, he could still have time to throw you out. If you keep on running as fast as you can, you will still have a chance to get to first base. Something like this happens in every game. If a runner stops running, he is almost sure to be put out. But alert base runners keep running, and some of them make it to first base safely. When you hit, don't watch the ball. Keep running as fast as you can until the umpire makes the call.

Base Runner on First

The first thing to do after reaching first base safely

WRONG WAY TO START: If you are on first base, you would need a couple of extra seconds to reach second starting from this side of the bag. This runner should be touching the inside of the bag with his left foot. In Little League baseball, you must keep tagging the bag until the pitched ball passes the hitter—then you can run.

is to look at your coach in the dugout or the coach behind first base, to see if he has any signals for you. He might want you to steal on the very next pitch. Or he might give the batter the bunt sign to try to sacrifice you over to second base into scoring position. If so, you've got to be ready to go: start fast, run hard, and slide if you need to. But before you start off, you must know what the signals are. If there are no signals, then you decide when and how you get to second base.

You also need to know the rule about how soon you can leave first base. Different groups have different rules. In "Boys Baseball" and some other groups, you can leave the base as soon as the pitcher has the ball. However, in "Little League," you must stay on the base from the time the pitcher steps on the rubber until the pitched ball has reached the hitter. If you leave too soon, the umpire will drop a red flag and can make you return to the base. You can't be called out for leaving too soon, but you can be made to return to the base. If the batter gets a good hit and reaches first base safely, the umpire will not make you return to first base because the hitter is there and you both can't be on first at the same time. But if you left first base too soon, and the catcher missed the ball, the umpire would make you return to first base, even though you had reached second base safely. So the best plan is to follow the rules—*don't leave the base until the ball has passed the hitter.*

The next thing you must know is whether to run or

not when the hitter hits the ball. It is sometimes hard to judge what to do. Most players say: "Go part way on a fly ball and run hard on a ground ball." This rule will cover most plays. When the batter knocks a fly ball, you have to get to second if the fielder misses it. You have to return to first base if he catches it. So the best thing to do is to go part way to second. If it is a long fly ball to the outfield you can go almost half-way. If the fielder catches the ball, he will have a long throw to first base, which you can usually beat. If the fielder misses the ball, you can surely make it to second while he is chasing the ball and throwing it.

If the hitter knocks a pop-up to the infield, you can go just a few steps, because if the infielder catches or misses the ball, he only has a short way to throw the ball. He can throw you out at first if he catches the ball or throw you out at second if he misses it. So you see, the best rule to follow on a fly ball is to go part way to second—almost half-way on a long fly ball and not so far on a short fly ball or a pop-up.

On ground balls, you have to run toward second. There is nothing else for you to do. The hitter is running to first. The only place you can go is to second. So run hard and fast to keep from getting caught in a double play. Slide into second if you need to. The second baseman might miss the ball if he is trying to watch your slide. So the rule is a good one— "Go part way on a fly ball and run on a ground ball."

While you are on first base, be alive . . . move

toward second . . . make the infield think you are going to run. Try to get the catcher or pitcher to throw the ball to the first baseman—he might miss it, letting you go on to second. But in doing this, make sure you stay close enough to the base to get back safely. You have to be on the bag when the pitcher is on the rubber.

Base Runner on Second

After you get to second base, with a runner behind you on first base, the rules are the same. You go part way on a fly ball and run on a ground ball. If the fly ball is caught, you have to beat the throw back to second. If the fly ball is missed you have to beat the throw to third. As it was at first base, you can take a lead until the pitcher gets on the rubber. Then you have to tag the base until the ball reaches the hitter. Leave the bag after every pitch to worry the infield. The catcher might miss the ball. The pitcher might even miss it as it comes back to him from the catcher. The infield might make a throw on you at second. If the ball gets through the second baseman, you might make it to third. Make sure you don't get too far off the base or you will be tagged out.

If there isn't a runner on first base, you do not need to run when the ball is hit. In this case, you shouldn't run unless you are sure you can make it to third safely. Don't leave the bag too soon. If there is no runner behind you, and you leave the bag too soon, the umpire can call you back to second, which might cost your team a run.

Base Runner Rounding Third

Coming to third base as a runner, you are ready to score a run—it might be the tying run or the winning run. As you are running to third from second, watch your coach at third base. He should be helping you with signals. Don't watch the ball . . . watch the coach. You will not need to turn around or turn your head to watch the ball. If you do, you won't run at full speed. The coach should use one of three hand signals:

A wave of his hand downward, which means to "hit the dirt" or slide into the base.

Hands held up in the air, which means "stand up," as you don't need to slide.

Hands rolling like a windmill, which means you should "keep running" and try to go on home. Hand signals are better than yelling, because sometimes the noise from the crowd is so loud you can't hear.

Base Runner on Third

Once you are at third base safely, don't take chances unless the coach or manager tells you to. If the pitcher throws a wild pitch and it gets away from the catcher, you might make it home if you go in sliding. In a tight game, call "time out" when you reach third base. Go over to talk with your manager to make sure you know what he wants you to do.

When you are at third, stay outside the foul line with your left foot on the edge of the bag. If you are inside the foul line, and the batter hits a ball toward third base which touches you, you will be called "out." If you are on the foul side of the line, you won't be called "out." As you run toward home plate, run just outside the foul line so you won't be called "out" for interference . . . just as at first base.

You should leave the bag after every pitch reaches the batter. This will give you two or three steps toward home plate which you might need if you have to go on home on a close play. You can safely take two or three steps each time the catcher gets the ball. You can get about as far off the bag as the third baseman. If he is close to the bag, he can make a play on you and perhaps tag you "out." If he is a long way from the bag, he will have a harder time tagging you. Never turn your back on the ball when you are off the base. Know where the ball is . . . make sure you can see it at all times. If you turn your back to the catcher when you *think* he is throwing the ball back to the pitcher, he might fake to the pitcher, then throw the ball to the third baseman. Walk backwards or sideways so you can watch the ball. If he throws the ball to the third baseman, then turn so you can run fast.

Watch the pitcher closely. Some pitchers will turn their back to third base as they get the ball from the catcher, and walk back to the mound without watching the runner at third base. If you are a very fast

HOME RUN, BUT OUT: Sometimes a batter hits the ball over an outfielder's head and runs all around the bases. But it doesn't count as a home run unless he touches home plate. Even though you get excited, don't crowd around home plate when a teammate gets a long hit. You might cover up the plate so he can't touch it. The umpire will call him out if the catcher gets the ball and steps on the plate before the runner does. Congratulate your teammate after he crosses the plate.

runner, you might be able to steal home before the pitcher can turn around to throw the ball.

With fly balls, play it differently on third base than

on first or second. If the batter could be the third out, or if the bases are loaded, you should run on any hit ball. On a long fly ball to the outfield, you should run back to third base as fast as you can and just touch the edge nearest home until the ball reaches the fielder, then run for home plate. You can usually make it to home plate safely after the fielder has caught the ball, *if you are on third base when he catches it.* If you take a lead from third base and have to go back to third *after* the ball is caught, you won't have time to make it home. So, we say: "Tag up on third on a long fly ball."

If you leave third base too soon, it could cost your team a score as the umpire might call you back. The other team will also be watching when you leave third base, hoping you leave too soon. So don't.

Crossing Home Plate

Don't slide home unless you have to. But slide if you are not sure you are going to be safe. Slide low, making sure you touch the plate. Home plate is not high, like the other bases. You have to make sure you slide over it, not against it. The most important thing is to make sure you touch the plate. It is easy to miss home plate. Boys do it all the time. They get excited about scoring a run and forget to touch home plate. Sometimes their teammates gather around home plate to pat them on the back, and the runner doesn't see the plate.

Runner Coming Home ◎ **101**

After you cross home plate your job is not done. You must act as the home plate coach if there is a runner following you who is on his way home.

Running All the Way Around

It is sad when a boy gets a home run then gets called "out," for missing the plate or one of the bases. When you are running the bases, make certain that you touch each of the bags as you pass. The best way is to try to use your right foot and step on the inside corner of each of the bases. When you cross home plate, step on the top of it . . . unless you are sliding . . . but make sure you touch it.

Another point to remember is that you cannot pass another runner in front of you. Do you think it isn't done? Even major league ball players do it. It is easy to have happen. You get a home run and get so excited that you forget the runner in front of you has stopped to watch the ball. If he lets you pass him, you will be called "out."

The Run-Down

If you get caught half-way between bases, what do you do? This is called getting caught in a "hot box" or a run-down. If the fielders do not make any mistakes, the runner will usually be tagged out. If they drop the ball or miss a throw, you may be safe, so help them make a mistake. Try to get them to throw the ball. The more often they throw it, the more chance they have to make a mistake, and the better chance you have to get to a base without being tagged. To make them throw the ball, always run away from the player with the ball. Don't turn your back on him. Always know which one has the ball and run away from him. Run sideways so you can watch the ball by just turning your head from side to side. While running back and forth, try to get close to one of the bases so you can slide into the base. If you can help the two fielders to get in each other's way, you will have a good chance to slide into a base safely.

Some Good Rules to Follow

There are lots of things to remember about running bases, aren't there? You have to know all the rules and be ready all the time. Here are a few more rules to remember:

When you get more than a single, run a short circle to the next base. Don't run in a great big circle. It slows you down.

Look at your manager or base coach after every pitch to see if he is giving a signal to tell you what to do.

Don't take a lead or try to run to the next base if there is a runner already on it.

Your lead from any base should not be further than the nearest baseman. If he is close, your lead can't be long.

SLIDE SITUATION: The second baseman, waiting for a
long throw from the catcher, is playing in front of the bag.
The runner can slide behind and away from the tag, on the
outfield side. But he should be flat on the ground already
—he has waited a moment too long to start his slide.

SLIDING

You should never slide in running the bases, unless you have to. But when you do slide, do it right—you won't hurt yourself and you won't hurt the other players. If you do it wrong, and if the playing field is hard around the bases, you might break a bone, or skin your legs or rear end. If the playing field is hard, wear a pair of old pants, with the legs cut off just above the knees, under your baseball pants. This will help prevent your skinning your legs, hips or seat.

The bases in most ball parks are tied down so they won't move. If you slide hard into them, with your knees stiff, you could hurt your legs. So learn how to slide safely.

There are three slides you should learn. The hook slide, the hand tag, and the straight-in or bent leg slide.

The Hook Slide

This is made either from the left or the right of the bag. If the ball is coming from the left, or if the baseman is in front of the bag, hook the right side of the bag. Let's use second base to show you how, because

HOOK SLIDE: The ball is in the glove waiting for the runner. But the runner may still be safe as he slides in, because the second baseman hasn't covered the ball with his other hand, and the runner's foot may knock it out.

most of the sliding is done here. Suppose you are running from first base toward second base. The shortstop is throwing the ball to second so the second baseman can tag you out. And the second baseman is in front of the bag. You should start your slide by landing on your seat while running fast. Double your right leg under your left leg. Your left leg should be pointed a little between left field and center field.

Don't aim your left foot at the bag. It will be your right toe which tags or hooks the right side of second base as your left leg and foot slide past the bag. Your body should be flat, or nearly flat, with your arms back over your head. This makes it harder for the second baseman to tag you. What you try to do is to slide under his tag.

If the second baseman is standing in back of the bag, on the center field side, you would try to tag the front of the bag, on the infield side. In this case, you would double your left leg under your right leg and tag the bag with the toe of your left foot as your right leg slides by the bag. Your right foot and toe would be pointed a little toward left field.

If you can't hook the bag with the foot which is bent under, there is another way to do it. If you want to touch the outside of the bag (the side on your right or the outfield side), start your slide with both legs stretched out, pointing toward the outfield. As you slide past the bag, double your left leg and hook the bag with your left toe. If you want to tag the inside of the bag (the one on your left or infield side), start your slide the same way, except, point your feet toward the infield side of the bag. As you slide past the bag, double your right leg and hook the bag with your right toe.

Either of these ways of using the hook slide is good. Use the one which you can do the best. Tag the bag with the toe of the top leg, or with the toe of the

HOOK SLIDE INTO THIRD BASE: The baseman will surely make the put-out as he has the ball in his glove and is covering it and the bag. The runner's slide is perfect— his legs are in the right position not to be hurt—but he is caught.

bottom leg. The important things to do in both cases are: (1) time your slide so that you stop just as you tag the bag, (2) aim your slide so that you slide to the side of the bag and touch it with just your toe, and (3) lie flat, to make it hard for the baseman to tag you.

If this slide is done right, you won't get any broken bones. The idea is to hit the bag with the toe of the leg which is doubled up ("bent') so that if you are sliding too fast, your leg will bend as the toe hits the bag. If you tag with the leg which is straight, the weight of your body and the speed of your slide might hurt or break your leg.

The Hand Tag

This slide is made very much like the hook slide. Let's use second base again to show you how. You are running toward second and the second baseman is standing so that his feet are in front of the bag—on the infield side. You should aim your slide so that both of your legs and feet are pointed slightly toward center field. You land on your seat with both legs stretched out in front of you. You keep your body flat on the ground, or nearly flat, with your arms back up and over your shoulders. You tag the bag with your left hand as you slide past. If the second baseman is standing in back of the bag—on the center field side—aim your slide toward left field so that you can tag the bag with your right hand as you slide past.

This slide also can be done without hurting yourself. Practice it. Wear some old clothes, with two pairs of pants and practice on the grass or in some soft sand.

The Bent Leg or Straight-In Slide

This slide is not as good to use as the others, because it is easier to hurt yourself while doing it. Use it only when you need to get on your feet fast so that

BENT LEG SLIDE: The runner is safe at third as he slides under the tag, but it's not the baseman's fault, as the throw is high.

you can go on to the next base. If you are running to second from first base, and the ball is coming in from shortstop on a close play, you might use the bent leg slide, because the second baseman might miss the ball. If he does, you can get up fast and go on to third base.

In this slide, you land on your seat with one leg doubled under you and the other stretched straight out, but not stiff. As you slide into the base, your front foot strikes the bag. Your slide doesn't stop . . . you keep it going, using your front foot and the bag to help you get up. You then are ready to run to third base. *This is a dangerous slide to use.* A lot of practice is needed in order to do it right. Wear old clothes and two pair of pants, and practice on sand or grass.

The Head-First Slide

The only time Little League ball players should use the head-first slide is when you have to dive back to a base after leaving it. The Little League rule book says you should not leave your base until the ball has passed the hitter. But you might leave it too soon. Or you might get too far from the base, and see a play being started on you. Then the quickest way to get back is to slide head-first to the base, touching it with your hand. *This is a dangerous slide to use*, because you might get hit in the head with the ball or kicked in the head by the baseman.

It should only be used for short slides of one or two feet. If you have to slide further than this, use one of the other slides. Dive back to the base only when you don't have the time to use one of the other slides.

Dress in old clothes, with two pairs of pants, get on the grass or some soft sand, and practice regularly. Use both your left and right toes to tag the bag. If you practice, you will be able to stop your slide just as your toe or hand touches the bag.

PLAYING THE OUTFIELD

Good baseball teams must have good outfielders. Outfielders must be able to catch ground balls as well as fly balls. Outfielders must be able to throw the ball to the infielders. If you want to be a good outfielder, here are some things you need to learn.

How to Throw the Ball Well

Practice throwing from the outfield so that the ball goes straight and fast without curving. To do this, you must throw much like a pitcher throwing a fast ball. Hold the ball with two fingers over two seams of the ball, just as if you were going to pitch a fast ball. Point your glove hand, arm, and shoulder toward the player who is going to catch the ball. Take a long step with your left foot (if you are left-handed, step with your right foot), and bring your throwing arm straight back over your shoulder. Using the muscles in your back and shoulder helps. Let the ball roll off the tips of your two fingers. Don't turn your wrist or throw the ball from the side. If you do, the ball will soon curve, and will not go straight.

Playing Right Field

If you are playing right field, you should always be ready to help the players near you. If the ball is batted or thrown toward the first baseman, you should run fast to get behind him. If he misses the ball, you can get it and throw it quickly, to keep the runner from going to the next base.

You should also help the center fielder. If he misses the ball and you are right behind him, you can get the ball and throw it to keep the runners from going to the next base.

Playing Left Field

If you are playing left field, you should always help the players near you. These are the third basemen, the shortstop and the center fielder. When a ball is hit or thrown toward one of these players, you should run fast to help him if he misses the ball.

Playing Center Field

The center fielder should be able to run fast. Usually the best fielder is chosen to play this position. The center fielder is really busy! If the right fielder misses the ball, the center fielder needs to back him up. If the left fielder misses the ball, the center fielder needs to be there to help him. The center fielder should also help the shortstop and the second baseman. So you see, he has to be fast, and needs a good throwing arm.

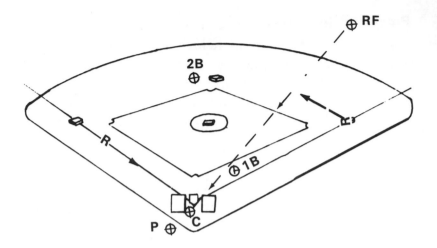

LF = Left Fielder   RF = Right Fielder
R = Runner   2B = Second Baseman
3B = Third Baseman   1B = First Baseman
C = Catcher   P = Pitcher

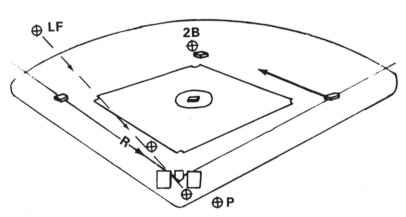

114 ◎ **Playing the Outfield**

Where Should You Throw the Ball?

One rule is: "Never throw behind the runner." Always throw the ball to the base in front of the runner. This will force him to stay where he is or go back to the base he just left. If you are in right field and get the ball when a runner is half-way between first and second base, you should throw the ball to second base. If there were runners on first and second base, you would try to get the ball to third base to keep the runner on second base from going to third base. Always throw in front of the *leading* runner.

If there is a runner on third base, you should try to throw the ball to the catcher to keep the runner from scoring a run.

Practice until you can throw the ball to reach the catcher about knee high. If you throw the ball too high in the air, it will take a long time to get to the plate and this will give the runner more time to get home.

Cut-Off Plays

The coach may want you to throw a "cut-off" ball, when throwing to the plate. If there are two runners on base and one is trying to reach home when the batter hits the ball to left field, the left fielder will throw the ball to the catcher. The third baseman will act as the "cut-off" man. He moves into the infield about 10 feet from the plate, so that he is between the left fielder and the catcher. If the runner will surely score from third base, the cut-off man (in this case, the third baseman) steps in the line of the throw, catches the ball and throws to try to stop the other runner from going to the next base.

If the ball is hit into right field, the first baseman acts as the cut-off man and moves 10 feet from home plate. If the ball comes from the right fielder too late for the catcher to make the tag at the plate, the cut-off man (in this case, the first baseman) takes the ball and is ready to stop the other runner from moving to the next base.

When the ball is hit into center field, the pitcher acts as the cut-off man. If the first or third baseman cannot leave his base, the pitcher could also be the cut-off man from throws coming in from right or left field.

If the catcher can see that the ball is going to get to him too late to make the tag, he yells: "Cut-off," and the cut-off man catches the ball. If the catcher doesn't yell, the cut-off man lets the ball go through. The ball then comes in on one bounce to the catcher.

It is better for an outfielder to throw straight to the catcher if he is trying to keep a runner from scoring.

For an outfielder to throw a cut-off ball, he must aim at the head of the cut-off player. If the fielder can't throw the ball straight to the catcher, he should practice throwing the cut-off ball so that it will bounce once before it reaches the catcher.

Get Rid of the Ball

Another rule is: "Don't hold the ball." A good outfielder watches the ball game very closely and knows every second where the runners are and what they will try to do. When he gets the ball, he knows where he has to throw it. When you get the ball, throw it as soon as you can. If you are not sure where to throw it, throw it to the infield player nearest you and in front of the runner.

If a runner has stopped between bases, it might be best to run with the ball straight toward the runner. Wait until you know which way he is going to run before you throw the ball. Or, if he is the leading runner and is waiting for you to throw (so he can run while the ball is in the air), you might run toward him to keep him on or near the base, then throw it to the nearest infield player.

Make sure when you throw the ball that you throw it right. You have seen many outfielders throw the ball poorly. If the baseman misses it, the runner goes to the next base. Sometimes runners can go all around the bases on bad throws.

Practice until you can make good throws. The best place to aim is at the knees, if a tag is to be made. This gives the baseman a chance to catch the ball and tag the runner. If you throw the ball at his chest, he has to stand up to catch the ball and then stoop too far to make the tag. A runner might slide under it. Catching

FLY BALL: Use your glove to shade your eyes from the sun, so you can follow the ball. Try to make the catch with your palms out and your gloved fingers pointing up at the level of your head or chest.

a ball thrown at his knees, the baseman can easily drop his glove to the runner making the slide and tag him. All other throws should be aimed at the chest, because this is the easiest place to catch the ball.

Catching the Fly Ball

Only practice can teach you how to catch a fly ball. The first thing you need to know is where the ball will land. This is called judging a fly ball. You should be able to tell where it will fall just as soon as the hitter hits it. You can then move to the place where it will land and be ready to catch it. Get to that place fast, and you will have a chance to move if the wind blows the ball to some other place. Very few fly balls come right to you. You have to judge where they will land and then go there.

You should never play right against the outfield fence, because you can't get to the short fly balls which land just behind the infield. It is best to play 10 to 12 feet from the fence. If the ball looks like it is going to be a home run, move back against the fence quickly and try to jump up and get it as it goes over the fence. Most of the fly balls do not reach the fence. If you play 10 or 15 feet away from it, on a normal Little League field, you can run forward to get those flies that fall just behind the infield. The exact place to play depends on your speed and the plans of the coach.

Try to catch the ball about even with your chest or head with the fingers of your glove pointed to the sky.

Have your other hand ready to reach around the glove to hold the ball in as it hits the glove. Some boys like to try the basket catch which Willie Mays made popular. This is catching the ball below your belt with the fingers of your glove pointed out, but this is not a good way for boys.

When you can hold your glove up, it will help keep the sun from your eyes while you watch the ball. Catching the ball around your chest or shoulders leaves you ready to make the throw. If you catch the ball low, you have to move your legs and body to get ready to throw.

Try to get under the ball. Be sure not to let it fall behind you. If you can't reach it, let it fall in front of you. Don't let it bounce over you or go through your legs. If you can't catch it, stop it.

Stopping the Ground Ball

Ground balls should never reach the fence. They should never go through the outfielders. You should always move toward ground balls—"charge" them. Never move back or wait for them. While you are taking one step, the runner can be taking two or three.

Place your arms, legs, and body so that if the ball misses your glove, your body will stop it. On most ground balls bend over a little. Bend your knees and keep your right foot (left if you are left-handed) back of the other foot 6 or 8 inches. Then, as you get the ball and stand up, you are ready to throw. Stop the ball, and throw it as soon as you can.

If a ground ball comes at you very fast, drop down on your right knee (left if you are left-handed) and block the ball with your glove and body. If the ball is rolling fast along the ground, hold your glove with the fingers on the ground. With the palm of your glove facing up, "scoop" up the ball as it rolls into the glove. If the ball is likely to bounce to your shoulders or head, turn your glove so the fingers point to the sky and catch the ball as it bounces. Either way, cover the front of your glove with your throwing hand as soon as the ball is in the pocket to keep it from jumping out. Make the throw as soon as you can.

Never turn your head or shut your eyes as a ground ball comes toward you. If you can't see the ball, it might bounce and hurt you. With your eyes open and looking straight at the ball, you can see it and knock it down or protect yourself with your glove. Some boys step to the side as they get a ground ball, but this is not a good way to do it. When the ball bounces, it may get past. Always charge a ground ball. Stay in front of it. Knock it down even if you can't catch it. Don't let it get by you.

Shifting for Left-Handed Hitters

Most boys bat right-handed and hit the ball to the left side of the field. So when a right-handed hitter is

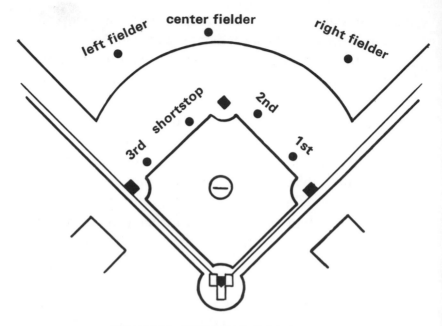

NORMAL FIELDING POSITIONS

at the plate, the outfielders should be in "normal" position. This means the left fielder should be back of and between the third baseman and the shortstop. The center fielder should be right behind second base and the right fielder behind and between the second baseman and the first baseman. If the hitter is a left-handed hitter, all the fielders should shift toward right field, as most left-handed hitters hit to right field. This should put the right fielder a little closer to the right field foul line and behind the first baseman. The center fielder should be a little toward right field. The left fielder should be nearer center field.

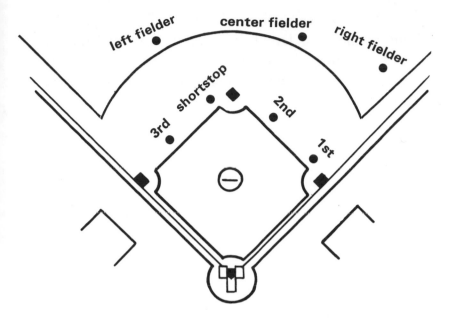

FIELDING POSITIONS FOR A LEFT-HANDED HITTER

Keep Your Mind on the Game

There may be innings when you have nothing to do in the outfield. Even if your body has nothing to do, keep your mind working. Keep thinking of the ball game. Watch every pitch and be ready. The hitter may send the ball right to you. See if you can "read" the signals the catcher is giving the pitcher. Yell to your teammates to encourage them. Talk to them about the game . . . how many outs . . . who is at bat . . . who is backing up the men on the infield. Coaches say to their outfielders: "Be in the ball game!" That means think about the game all the time. Don't listen to the crowds or talk to anyone but your teammates. Don't be thinking of anything but the ball game. Be listening and watching for instructions from your catcher, pitcher or your coach at all times.

PLAYING THE INFIELD

The infielders are not only the first baseman, second baseman, third baseman and shortstop, but the pitcher, and the catcher too. They should read this chapter. They all must know the game very well. They must be able to catch fly balls, line drives, and ground balls—and throw well. Most of the game of baseball is played by the infield. This is where most of the action is.

Playing First Base

Most of the outs in a game are made by throwing the ball to the first baseman. He must be able to catch the ball well. Many coaches like to use boys who are left-handed as first basemen because they wear their gloves on their right hand. Because the glove is on their right hand, they can catch balls which go between them and the second baseman easier than a right-handed boy. So, if you are left-handed and especially if you are tall, try first base. You might like it.

THE RIGHT WAY TO PLAY FIRST BASE on an infield grounder. The first baseman is stretching toward the shortstop as he keeps the edge of his rear foot on the bag. The runner is tagging the outside corner of the bag with his left foot. Is he out or safe?

The first thing to know about playing first base is that you have to reach out and stretch often to catch the ball. To do this, if you are a right-hander put your right heel or foot on the inside corner of the bag.

If you are left-handed, use your left heel or foot. Now take a long step with your other foot toward the infielder who is going to throw the ball to you. Aim your mitt or glove at him. You are now ready to catch the ball.

Some boys play first base with their foot right in the middle of the bag. This is wrong. The runner might step on your foot as he crosses the bag, and this might hurt you or the runner. You might trip each other and even break a leg.

As you catch the ball, push your foot back against the base to make sure you touch it. The reason you stretch toward the boy throwing the ball is to shorten his throw. This helps the throw beat the runner to the base.

Sometimes when an infielder throws the ball to the first baseman, he throws it wild. So the first baseman must be ready to jump high, or move to right or left to get the ball. Sometimes the ball is thrown low in the dirt, and it comes in like a ground ball. A good first baseman can always scoop the ball out of the dirt. You must try to stop all balls which come to you—don't let them get by you. If you can't hold your foot on the base and catch the ball at the same time, take your foot off the base and go after the ball.

The next thing you need to know is where you play when you are not catching batted balls thrown to you. Your job as first baseman is to "play the bag."

THE WRONG WAY: (Left) The first baseman is standing on top of the bag. He is trying to catch a ball thrown around the runner, who is on the wrong side of the foul line. (Right) As the first baseman is playing the middle of the bag, the runner is forced to use his body to push his way to the bag. This could cause one or both boys to be hurt.

You have to make the catch to get the runner out. So you can't move very far away from the bag. Let the second baseman take most of the fly balls and ground balls that go between you and him. You should play back of the base path about a foot and 5 to 6 feet in from the bag most of the time. If the hitter is left-handed, he is more likely to hit the ball right over first base than a right-handed batter. So you need to play closer to the foul line for left-handed hitters.

Balls bunted down the first base line always give the first baseman, the catcher and the pitcher trouble. If the bunt is close to the plate, the catcher should get it, and the first baseman should stay on the bag to take the throw. The first baseman should never go after the ball unless he knows the pitcher or second baseman can run to first base to take the throw.

If you field a ball hit to you and throw first to second base to get a runner, try to throw to the outside of the base path, so you won't hit the runner. If you hit him, you not only might hurt him, but he would be safe. The second baseman would not be able to catch the ball to make the out. After throwing to second, rush back to your bag to take the return throw for a double play.

The first baseman also has to catch fly foul balls hit near first base. If you catch a foul ball, remember the runners on base may run as soon as you catch the ball, so be ready to make a throw after the catch.

Playing Second Base and Shortstop

The second baseman and the shortstop work as a team. When a right-handed hitter is at the plate, expect that he will hit the ball between the shortstop and the third baseman. So the shortstop plays to the

SECOND BASEMAN COVERING FIRST BASE: On a bunt, the first baseman comes in to field the ball and the second baseman moves over quickly to take the throw. Notice that he stands on the infield side of the bag, using his glove as a target and giving the runner a clear path on the chalk line.

back edge of the base path and 8 to 10 feet away from second base. The second baseman plays 4 to 6 feet from second base and at the back edge of the base path. The second baseman will have to take any fielder's throw to second base to put the runner out.

If the hitter at the plate is left-handed, the shortstop plays a little closer to second base, about 4 to 6 feet from the bag. He plans to take any throw to put the runner out. The second baseman plays a little closer to first base (about 8 to 10 feet from second base). He has to get any ball that might be hit between first and second bases.

The second baseman and the shortstop should catch all the fly balls they can get without running into another fielder or each other. Remember that it is much easier to catch a fly ball if you are running forward to it than backwards. So the second baseman and the shortstop should catch all fly balls which come between their positions and the pitcher's mound. They should also catch those that fall close to second base. Let the outfielders catch those which go over their heads more than 10 or 12 feet.

The second baseman and the shortstop must back up each other whenever possible. Yes, the outfielders are backing up both of them, but it is good to have everybody helping. If the shortstop can run fast, he might be able to back up the third baseman. He might also catch a fly ball or foul fly back of third base if the third baseman can't get to it.

If the game is close, and there is a runner on third base, the shortstop and second baseman must play "in"—that is, they take their places at the front edge of the base path. This will shorten their throw to the plate if the runner on third tries to score. Often a runner can be thrown out at the plate on a ground ball to the infield. With two out, the infielders should move back a little and play for the third out on a fly ball or a ground ball and a throw to first base.

THIRD BASEMAN READY TO TAG: Bent over slightly, he waits for the ball to be thrown to him. He can make the tag without injury to himself or the runner. In this case, the sliding runner has beaten the throw.

Playing Third Base

To play third base, the "hot corner," you must be able to stop hard-hit ground balls and catch "hot" line drives. You must have a strong arm so you can throw hard to first base. When a right-handed hitter is at the plate, you need to play at the back edge of the base path and 5 to 6 feet from third base. When a left-handed hitter is at the plate, you have to play a little closer to second base to help the shortstop. If the hitter bunts the ball down the third base line where the pitcher or catcher can't get it, it is up to the third baseman to get the ball and make the throw to first base. A high fly ball over third base, which does not reach the outfield, has to be caught by the third baseman. A fly ball which comes near third base should be caught by the third baseman for an out. Remember, when there are runners on base, and you catch a foul ball, they can run after the catch. So be ready to throw as soon as you catch the ball.

With a runner on third base, and the game close, the third baseman should move to the front edge of the base path to shorten the throw to home plate, so the runner can be thrown out. With two out, he should move back to his normal position and be ready to make an out on a fly ball or a throw to first on a ground ball.

Call for Fly Balls

Many fly balls are missed because two or more boys go after it at the same time. When you think you can get it, start yelling: "I've got it! I've got it!" and keep yelling until you catch the ball. If it is not coming to you, try to get it, but if you hear someone else yelling: "I've got it! I've got it!" and you are in his area, stop and let him take it. Outfielders should do this also.

Fielding Ground Balls

Ground balls usually come at you faster in the infield than they do in the outfield. So an infielder has to be faster in handling ground balls. The most important thing is to stop the ball. Don't let it get through to the outfield, as that usually lets runners go to the next base and perhaps score a run. Here are some suggestions which might help:

ALWAYS BE READY FOR THE BALL. When a hitter is at the plate, expect that the ball is going to come to you. Stand, well balanced, on both feet, legs bent a little at the knees—arms and hands in front of you. Rest your hands on your knees, if you want, but watch the ball and the hitter carefully. Be ready if the ball comes anywhere in your direction.

ALWAYS TRY TO GET IN FRONT OF THE BALL. If you can get in front of the ball, you have a much better chance to catch it or knock it down. Very few balls will come straight at you. You usually have to move to right or left to get the ball. If the ball is not hit very hard, you can run in towards it. But if the ball has been hit hard, you have to judge where the ball is going and run fast to get to that spot before the ball does. The main thing is to get in front of it.

ALWAYS "CHARGE" THE BALL. There are very few times when you should back up to take ground balls. Most of the time you should "charge" them. It is easier to run forward than it is to run backwards. Try it. Running backwards you might stumble and get

PICKING UP A GROUNDER: Notice how an infielder places his right foot a few inches back and to the side of his left foot. This places him in a good position to rise up and throw the ball in the shortest possible time. Most ground balls should be fielded like this.

Fielding Ground Balls ◎ 135

off-balance. When you are running forward, you can watch the ball better and also catch it easier. Another reason for charging the ball is that you can get to the ball faster and have a better chance of throwing the runner out. If you wait for the ball to come to you, or if you back up, you might not have enough time to make the play on the runner.

WATCH THE "HOP" OF THE BALL. A ground ball usually hops or bounces. As it comes toward you, watch it carefully. Watch how it hops. If it is taking little hops, you should field it close to the ground with the fingers of your glove pointing down, palm up, and your throwing hand ready to hold the ball in the glove as it hits the pocket. If the ball is just skimming along the ground, you might try dropping to one knee like an outfielder and stopping it with your body. If the ball is taking big hops or bounces it will probably be taking big hops when it reaches you. Run toward it and try to catch it at the top of a hop or bounce. To do this you should catch it in your glove with the fingers pointing up and your throwing hand ready to trap it in your glove.

GET IN THE RIGHT POSITION. The crouch position is best for balls which are lower than your belt, especially those which are taking small, fast hops —just skimming over the top of the ground. Have your right foot (left foot if you are left-handed) 6 to 8 inches in back of your other foot. Then your feet will be in the right position to throw after you get the

PICKING UP A GROUNDER (rear view)

ball. When you have the ball, raise up, take a quick step, and throw without wasting time. You usually field the ball with the fingers of your glove pointing down, palm up, when using the crouch position.

The position to use when fielding ground balls that take large, high hops is the stand-up position. You field the ball with the fingers of your glove pointing up and your feet spread apart slightly for good balance. Your right foot (left foot if you are left-handed) should be a little farther back than the other foot. As in the crouch position, you can get ready to throw without taking extra steps. On ground balls that are higher than your belt, use the stand-up position.

Some boys develop a bad habit of sidearming the ball. They step to the side of it and try to field it in their glove to the side. In the crouch and stand-up positions, your body is behind your glove so that if you miss the ball you can still stop it. In the sidearm position, if you miss the ball, it could go all the way to the outfield fence. Forget about the sidearm position in fielding ground balls.

ALWAYS MAKE STEADY THROWS after you field the ball. You sometimes see major league ball players throw the ball while they are in the air or moving fast. This is not good for boys. Be a good Little Leaguer first, then think about throwing like the major leaguers do. The best way for Little Leaguers is to make sure you have the ball and then throw from a throwing position. It will do little good if you make a beautiful stop on a ground ball and make a bad throw. Try to come to a complete halt before you make the throw.

BE READY FOR THE NEXT PLAY. Making a good stop on the ball is not enough. Keep thinking all the time.

STOPPING A "HOT" GROUNDER: Drop down on one knee and use your leg and body to help stop a hard-hit ball.

Know where the base runners are and what they are going to do as soon as you get the ball. Be alert! Be ready for the next play. Watch the ball all the way to your glove. Forget about the runner until you have the ball, then know where to throw it.

When you are playing "catch" with someone, have him throw you a few ground balls. Practice charging them. Try some slow ones and some hot ones. Get so you can field them all.

Fielding Ground Balls ⊚ **139**

Catching Fly Balls

Infielders should catch fly balls just like outfielders. One of the most difficult things for boys to learn is when to take the fly ball and when to let the player next to you take it. If the fly ball is coming to your position, you take it. Don't wait for any one else, but make sure you yell: "I got it!! I got it!!" and keep yelling until you catch the ball. If the ball is a little out of your area, try for it, but if you hear the player next to you yelling "I got it"—let him have it.

When a fly ball gets lost in the sun, learn to shield your eyes with your glove. Judge where the ball will land, get under it, and wait for it. Try to catch the ball about even with your chest and shoulders. Use both hands. Catch the ball in your glove, but have your throwing hand ready to trap the ball in the glove as it hits.

Throwing the Ball in the Infield

All throws in the infield but one are usually short, fast throws. One of the hardest is the short throw when you are only 6 to 8 feet away from the player who is to catch the ball. If you throw it hard, he will miss it, because he won't have time to move his glove. If you throw it easy, the runner might beat the throw. The best way is to "flip" the ball to him if you are close—not too hard, and not too easy. Use the same wrist motion as you do when you throw, but don't throw hard.

You can't take a big stride like an outfielder. You have to take a short step. Also you throw "from your ear"—you pull your arm back only as far as your ear. Aim at the baseman's chest, unless he has to make a tag, then aim for his knees. Sometimes you may have to use a sidearm throw, but don't use it unless you have to, because it is not easy to catch. It is also hard to throw. Use it when you don't have enough time to throw the way you usually do. Sometimes, on double plays, when the runner is in the base path and you have to throw around him, the sidearm throw is necessary.

Making the Tag

As the runner slides into second or third base, you must try to tag him without getting hurt or hurting the other player. Your feet and legs may get hurt if you stand in the wrong place. And if you tag the runner in the wrong place, you may hurt him. You can place your feet on either side of the bag, but not in front of it or behind it. If your feet are in front of the bag, the runner cannot slide into the bag without sliding into your feet. If you have your feet behind the bag, you will have a hard time trying to tag him before he slides in.

There are two ways to do it. One way is to face the runner with one foot on each side of the bag. This gives you a good position to make the tag. If the pitcher is throwing to you, it is not hard to catch the ball in this position. But if the shortstop is throwing the ball to you at second base, you have to turn your body to get it. You might have to wait until after you get the ball to take this stance over second base. When you have the ball, place your glove with the ball in it on the ground in front of the base. Let the runner slide into it. You must hold the ball in your glove with one hand, so the runner won't kick it out of your glove. This position works best at third base because you can catch most balls thrown to you without turning. It makes the runner slide straight toward the base.

For second base, you might try another way. Try standing with both feet on the outside of the bag (the center field side). Face the player who is going to throw you the ball. He should throw the ball at your knees. After you catch it, turn your body to the left, and lay the glove, with the ball in it, in front of the sliding runner. Let him tag himself out. Keep your hand on the ball to keep it in the glove, and let him tag the back of your glove. If he sees you standing in this position, he might try to slide to the infield side of the bag and use a hook or hand tag. In either case, you let him slide into your glove and tag himself.

Another way is to stand so that both feet are on the inside (infield side) of the bag. You make the tag the same way. Turn to your left and drop your glove in front of the sliding runner. Keep the ball away from his feet or hands. He might kick it or knock it out of your hands.

Take your glove away just as soon as the tag has been made, so you don't drop the ball as you both get up. Never try to tag a sliding runner on the body, shoulders or head. His feet will beat you to the bag. Always try to make the tag on his feet, or his hand if he is making a hand tag. You have to tag low, or he may slide under your glove.

The Double Play

Most double plays are made from second base to first base. The second baseman and the shortstop are the ones who start most of the double plays. The runner on first base has to reach second—he is "forced." You must tag second base before the forced runner gets to it. Then you throw the ball to the first baseman to beat the batter.

As you catch the ball, tag the bag with your rear foot, then push with the same foot as you take a step to throw to first base. Whether you are on the inside or outside of the bag, take a short step to touch the bag with your right foot, then step toward first base with your left foot as you throw. If you have to run across the bag with the ball, push off the side of the bag with your right foot as you cross, then throw to first. But don't throw the ball into the runner as he comes to second base. No fielder may interfere with a runner.

You should coach your infield teammates to throw at your chest. It is easier to catch the ball this way for a double play. When you have to make a tag on a sliding runner, the throw should be aimed at your knees.

The Run-Down or Hot Box

If the infielders play right, runners in the hot box should be caught every time. The only way a runner can get out of the hot box is when an infielder makes a mistake. These are the things the fielders have to do:

When a run-down develops, close the gap. This means that the boy who has the ball must chase the runner back to the other baseman as quickly as he can, so that long throws are not needed. A runner in the box cannot be tagged out while the ball is being thrown a big distance between the two basemen. You have to get close to make the tag.

The runner should be chased back to the bag he left. If you chase him forward, and make a mistake, he might be able to go on to the next base.

Never leave a base uncovered. There should be four players on each run-down play. Two boys should be throwing and two more should be ready to take over if the runner gets away. The back-up boys should also be ready to get the ball if it is overthrown and keep the runner from getting an extra base. Only

A HOT BOX may start when a runner takes too long a lead off third base as the hitter swings. The third baseman moves to the bag to take a pick-off throw from the catcher. If the runner doesn't get back in time he will be caught in a run-down.

two boys work the run-down at one time. But there should be one other boy near each of the bases to step in and take over if he is needed.

Make all your throws on the outside or inside of the base path. If you hit the runner, or just his arm or hand, he will probably be safe because the boy you are throwing to may not be able to catch the ball.

When you are ready to catch the ball, give your teammate a target with your glove on the outside or inside of the base path.

Make soft throws wherever you can. The closer you get to the player who is to catch the ball, the harder it will be for him to catch it.

Don't make any more throws than you need to. Each time you make a throw, you have a chance of making an error . . . throwing the ball away or missing the catch. If you have a choice, run with the ball rather than throw it.

Use the fake throw when you get close to the runner. After a runner has made you throw two or three times, you can fake a throw and he'll turn and run into you, tagging himself out.

Get Ready for the Next Play

After you have made a good catch, or a good tag for an out, look for another play. A smart base runner will be watching you. If you hold the ball, or toss it to another player, or throw it into the dugout, thinking it is the last out when it isn't, he will run for the next base. You have to be awake . . . think of the ball game every minute.

All Infielders Stretch

The first baseman is the one who needs to stretch most often, but the other infielders should also be able to do this. When you need to make a force out on a runner by keeping one foot on the bag, it is always better to stretch toward the boy throwing the ball to you. This shortens the throw and might help the throw beat the runner to the base.

Always Watch the Base Runner's Feet

As the other team runs around the bases, don't watch the ball or the crowd . . . watch their feet and make sure they touch each base. If they miss one, wait until they have stopped running, or the play is over, then call for the ball to be thrown to the bag they missed. When the bag is tagged, the umpire will call the runner out, if he really missed touching the base.

THE TEN COMMANDMENTS OF BASEBALL

It is said that many years ago the manager of the New York Yankees wrote 10 rules for baseball players to help them play better ball. They might help you. You may not understand all the words, so we have tried to explain what each of them means.

1. *Nobody ever becomes a ball player by walking after the ball.* No one likes to see ball players who do not run. If you don't have enough strength to run, you shouldn't try to play baseball. If you don't run, your coach will think you don't like to play baseball. Move fast all the time. Even in practice and between innings, while you are moving on and off the field, you should run. It saves time and it helps build team spirit.

2. *You will never become a .300 hitter unless you take the bat off your shoulder.* This means you should always be ready to hit the ball. At the plate, if you stand with your bat resting on your shoulder, you can't

get ready to swing quick enough to hit the ball when the pitcher throws it.

3. *An outfielder who throws back of the runner is locking the barn door after the horse is stolen.* If a runner starts from first base to second after a fly is caught, and the outfielder throws the ball to first, he is wasting a throw. If you throw to second, you have a chance to catch the runner, or at least force him back to first base.

4. *Keep your head up and you may not have to keep it down.* People hang their head down, and won't look at others, when they make a foolish mistake. If you are wide awake, and know what is going on in the game, you won't make a foolish mistake. You have to keep your mind on the game every minute. You have to know who is at bat, where you should throw the ball if you get it, and what to do with the ball if it comes to you. Keep wide awake . . . don't dream or be thinking of something else when you are playing baseball.

5. *When you start to slide . . . SLIDE.* You can't change your mind in the middle of a slide. When you slide, you have to do it fast, and do it right, or you could break a leg. When you start to play baseball, play it hard. Don't "goof off."

6. *Do not alibi for bad hops. Anyone can field good ones.* Even the best ball players make mistakes. One major league ball player dropped two fly balls in one inning in a World Series game. He didn't blame any-

body but himself. If you miss a ground ball, don't blame it on the ball or the field. If it takes a bad bounce, and you miss it, no one will blame you. It happens to everybody. But don't try to blame someone else. Just try to do better next time.

7. *Always run them out. You never can tell.* When you hit a little pop fly or a soft grounder to the infield, try to make it to first base. Don't stop running. The other player might miss the ball, or throw it wild to the first baseman. The first baseman might drop the ball.

8. *Don't quit.* You can never tell what will happen in a ball game. You must never think you are going to lose. It makes no difference where you play . . . pitcher, catcher, or right field . . . you must always help your teammates. Don't let them quit. Don't say things that will make them quit. Say things that will help them play better. No one likes a boy who quits. Keep playing.

9. *Don't find fault with the umpire. You can't expect him to be as perfect as you are.* A player never wins fights with an umpire. He might make a wrong call or may not know the rule, but you as a player can't win a fight with him. If he doesn't know the rule, your coach or manager can talk to him about it, and even go to the league officials, and get the ruling changed, but *you* cannot do it. The umpire is doing the best job he can. He is honest and will be as fair as he can. Don't make it harder for him by fighting

with him. When you know baseball so well that you do not make mistakes, then you can be an umpire.

10. *A pitcher who hasn't control hasn't anything.* If the pitcher can't throw strikes, he isn't pitching well. A pitcher who gets angry and can't control his temper, can't play good ball. You need to want to win, and you need to play hard at all times, but if you get into a fight, you are no good to the team. All players need to have control.

GLOSSARY

BASKET CATCH: Catching a fly ball with your glove held below your chest, and the back of your hand turned to the ground, as if using the glove as a basket. It is not a very good way for boys to catch the ball.

BATTER'S BOX: The area on each side of home plate where the batter stands while he is hitting the ball. It is 3 feet wide and $5\frac{1}{2}$ feet long. White chalk is usually used to draw the batter's box on the ground.

BREAK: Another word for "curve." When a ball is thrown in a certain way, it looks like it curves or changes direction just before it gets to the hitter. When it does, we say that it "breaks."

BUNT: When a batter just taps the ball or pushes the bat into the ball to make it roll in front of the plate where the fielders and the pitcher and catcher have a hard time getting it, it is called a bunt.

CHAIR POSITION: The right position for a catcher to catch the ball as the pitcher throws it: he looks almost as if he is sitting on the edge of a chair.

CHARGE THE BALL: To run toward the ball as it is coming to you. Good fielders always charge a soft hit ball rather than wait for it to get to them.

CHANGE OF PACE: When a pitcher throws several fast balls then throws a slow ball, it is called a change of pace and helps fool the hitter.

CHOKE UP: When you hold a bat with 1 or 2 inches between your bottom hand and the end of the bat it is called choking-up. This helps you to swing the bat faster. It is good to use when your bat is a little too long or when you are facing a fast ball pitcher.

CONTROL: When a pitcher can make the ball go where he wants it to go, he has control. When you have "control" you can throw strikes almost every time. You can throw low strikes to tall boys, and high strikes to small boys. You can make the ball go over the inside or the outside of the plate.

CUT: When you swing the bat at the ball it is called a cut. It makes no difference if you hit the ball or miss it, it is called a cut.

DUGOUT: This is where the players not on the field stay during the ball game. Sometimes it is made by digging a hole in the ground and sometimes a dugout is built on top of the ground.

FIELDER'S CHOICE: When there is a runner on base and the batter hits the ball to the infield, the boy who fields the ball has to decide whether to try to get the base runner out or throw out the batter. The fielder usually tries to make the easiest play and get the base runner out. The hitter then gets on first base by a "fielder's choice." It is not counted as a hit.

FOLLOW-THROUGH: When you hit the ball with the bat, you should not try to stop the bat . . . let it swing on around. This is follow-through. If you try to stop the bat as you hit the ball, you lose some of the power in your swing. This is what happens when you bunt the ball. You don't use any follow-through when you bunt.

FORCE PLAY: A runner on first base has to go to second on a ground ball. Also a runner on any base has to go to the next base when a runner is on base behind him. This is called a "force" situation. All the baseman needs to do is beat the runner to the base with the ball. He doesn't have to tag the runner . . . he can get him out by just stepping on the base with the ball.

FOUL LINE: A white line drawn on the ground from home plate straight to right field over first base and from home plate straight to left field over third base. If a ball lands on the outside of this line it is a foul ball.

HOT BOX: When a runner gets caught between two bases and the infielders try to tag him out, he is in the hot box.

INSIDE PITCH: When the pitcher throws the ball so that it comes close to the hitter, it is called an inside pitch.

LABEL: People who make baseball bats put their name on the bat by painting or branding it with a hot iron. This is called the label or brand.

LEAD: A runner in Little League baseball should take one or two short steps from his base each time the pitcher pitches the ball. This is called a lead.

LITTLE LEAGUE: There are many baseball leagues for boys. The one which is the most widely known is "Little League Baseball," with headquarters in Williamsport, Pennsylvania. There are also Little League teams in Mexico, Japan, China and other parts of the world. The name "Little League" is so popular that almost everyone uses it when talking about all baseball activities of boys aged 9 to 12.

OUTSIDE PITCH: When a pitcher throws the ball so that it crosses the side of the plate opposite the side where the hitter is standing, it is an outside pitch. If a batter stands too far from the plate, the pitcher may throw an outside pitch which the batter can't reach, and it may be over for a strike.

PIVOT: To pivot means to turn. If you are standing on one foot and turn around on that foot, that is the pivot foot, the one you turn on. The pitcher's pivot foot is the foot he uses to push against the rubber as he releases the ball. If you are right-handed this will be your right foot. If you are left-handed it will be your left foot.

POP-UP: When you hit the baseball and it goes into the air just a little . . . making it possible for an infielder to catch it easily, it is called a pop-up fly ball.

RELEASE POINT: The point at which a pitcher lets go of the ball, or releases it. If he releases it too soon, it will go too high to be a strike. If he releases it too late, the ball will go too low to be a strike. A pitcher must practice so he knows exactly where to release the ball so that it goes where he wants it to go.

RUBBER: The rubber plate on the pitcher's mound where the pitcher stands. It is 4 inches wide and 18 inches long.

THE LABEL OR BRAND appears this way on all bats. It is usually burned in with a hot iron.

SACRIFICE: If there is a runner on first base and you are batting, the coach might tell you to sacrifice. This means that you should try to hit the ball towards the first-base side of the infield and make the infielder throw the ball to first base to get you out, letting the runner go safely to second base. This would put him in a position to score. Often, a bunt is a type of sacrifice.

SEAMS: A cover of a baseball is made from two pieces of leather, sewn on with strong thread. Where these two pieces of leather are sewn together there is a seam. Good pitchers use a seam to help them throw the ball better.

SHIFT: To move a little or change positions. Fielders will often shift to their left for a left-handed hitter because he will usually hit the ball toward the first-base side of the field. They shift toward third base for a right-handed hitter.

SIGNALS: The catcher and pitcher use finger signals to talk with each other so that no one else knows what they are saying. The catcher holds one, two, three or four fingers in a certain way to suggest to the pitcher what kind of a pitch he thinks would work best on the batter. The coach in the dugout might use a signal to tell his players what he wants them to try, without letting the other team know about it.

SPIN: When a baseball is spinning, it is turning around very fast. All pitches except the knuckle ball should turn or spin as they move through the air. This helps them to go straight.

"STEP IN THE BUCKET": When batting, you should take a very *short* step or stride straight toward the pitcher as you swing. If a right-handed batter takes a *long* step toward third base, he is "stepping in the bucket." You can't hit very well if you step in the bucket.

STRIKE ZONE: The area that crosses home plate between the armpits and the knees of the hitter. It is approximately 18 inches wide × 30 inches high, depending on the height of the batter.

TAG UP: The runner on base must be touching or "tagged up" on the base at the moment the outfielder catches a fly ball. If he leaves the base before the outfielder catches the ball, he can be put out if a fielder can get the ball to the base before he can get back to it. You should always tag up on a fly ball except when there are two outs.

TARGET: The pitcher usually uses the catcher's outstretched mitt as a target and tries to hit it.

TIME OUT: When a player or a coach calls "time" or "time out," the umpire stops the game and no one can run or score. If a boy is injured, it is always best to call "time" to stop the game. You have to wait until the proper moment, however. For example, if a runner is scoring you can't call "time" to keep him from scoring. You have to wait until the play is completed, or "dead," and then you can call "time."

WARM UP: When your father starts the car on a cold morning, he usually lets it run for a moment or two so the motor can warm up, before he drives off at a fast speed. Your muscles, too, have to be warmed up a little before they can work their best. Athletes know this and will warm up their muscles. Pitchers in baseball know that they have to warm up their pitching arms before they can throw hard. If they don't, their arms get sore. So to warm up, you see, means to get ready.

WILD PITCH: When a pitcher throws the ball so wide of the strike zone that the catcher can't get it, and it goes past him into the backstop or the bleachers, it is called a wild pitch.

INDEX

Index ⊙

WARM UP for LITTLE LEAGUE BASEBALL

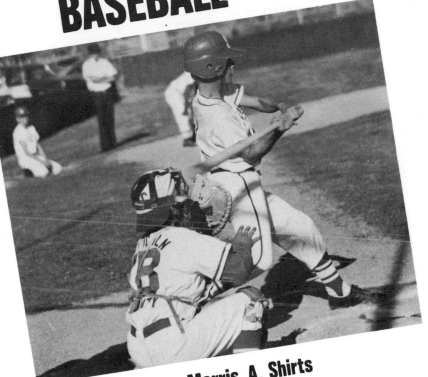

By Dean Morris A. Shirts
of Southern Utah State College

PHOTOGRAPHS BY THE AUTHOR

STERLING PUBLISHING CO., INC.   **NEW YORK**

OTHER BOOKS OF INTEREST

Book of Baseball Records
Guinness Sports Record Book
101 Best Action Games for Boys

ATHLETIC INSTITUTE SERIES

Baseball — Siebert & Vogel
Basketball — Allen
Girls' Basketball — Barnes
Girls' Gymnastics — Wachtel
Gymnastics — Loken
Table Tennis — Wasserman
Tumbling & Trampolining — Loken
Wrestling — Peery & Umbach

Third Printing, 1972
Copyright © 1971 by
Sterling Publishing Co., Inc.
419 Park Avenue South, New York, N.Y. 10016
Manufactured in the United States of America
Library of Congress Catalog Card No.: 70-151708
ISBN 0–8069– 4044 –1
4045 –X